GOD ON THE PLANET OF THE APES
UNCOVERING THE LESSONS OF THE LAWGIVER

DANN MICHALSKI

God on the Planet of the Apes: Uncovering the Lessons of the Lawgiver

Copyright © 2023 by Dann Michalski. All rights reserved.

Cover photo by GordonImages

ISBN 979-8-8690-2430-5

All Scripture quotations are taken from the *Holy Bible*, New International Version ®, NIV ®, Copyright © 2011 by Biblica, Inc.™

Dedicated to my dad

CONTENTS

INTRODUCTION 1

CHAPTER 1: PLANET OF THE APES 6

CHAPTER 2: BENEATH THE PLANET OF THE APES 18

CHAPTER 3: ESCAPE FROM THE PLANET OF THE APES 29

CHAPTER 4: CONQUEST OF THE PLANET OF THE APES 40

CHAPTER 5: BATTLE FOR THE PLANET OF THE APES 50

CHAPTER 6: PLANET OF THE APES 60

CHAPTER 7: RISE OF THE PLANET OF THE APES 71

CHAPTER 8: DAWN OF THE PLANET OF THE APES 82

CHAPTER 9: WAR FOR THE PLANET OF THE APES 93

CONCLUSION 105

BIBLIOGRAPHY 111

INTRODUCTION

"Beware the beast man, for he is the Devil's pawn. Alone among God's primates, he kills for sport or lust or greed. Yea, he will murder his brother to possess his brother's land. Let him not breed in great numbers, for he will make a desert of his home and yours. Shun him. Drive him back into his jungle lair, for he is the harbinger of death." —Sacred Scrolls

I love Planet of the Apes. Ever since my dad first introduced me to the films in my childhood, I haven't been able to get enough—and I've tried. It began with buying a collector's boxset of the original five films on VHS, then (when I was ready) I read the novelizations and eventual Pierre Boulle's original novel. And when that wasn't enough, I bought the action figures and comics.

At first it was the apes that I loved. Something about that makeup and the whole look of the world fascinated me. It was equal to anything from Star Wars or Star Trek (which I was also a fan of). But talking apes held more of a fascination than aliens. It was more real—at least to a child. And the hideous mutants *Beneath the Planet of the Apes* gave me nightmares. For years I was unable to watch the unmasking scenes.

When I grew older and became more of a cinephile, I started to appreciate the *Apes* films on a whole new level. The caliber of actors was quite impressive: Charlton Heston, Roddy McDowall, Kim Hunter, Claude Akins, Ricardo Montalbán, and John Huston—

just to name a few. And the screenwriters included *Twilight Zone* creator Rod Serling and the writer of the James Bond classic *Goldfinger* Paul Dehn. The directors were A-list as well: *Patton*'s Franklin J. Schaffner, Ted Post (director of the Clint Eastwood classic *Hang 'Em High*), and J. Lee Thompson (of *The Guns of Navarone*). Even the music was done by first-rate composers; such as Jerry Goldsmith and Leonard Rosenman.

At first glance the *Apes* films may appear to be cheap, low-budget B-movies—yet they were anything but. They featured some of Hollywood's top talent, and it showed—becoming one of the top franchises of the time. And when the franchise was later revived, it once again drew leading directors and actors.

One of the things that made the franchise so impactful was its social commentary. The films reflected the social issues of the day; tackling such topics as race, class, and nuclear war. Some of it was subtle and some of it was blatantly obvious (hit you across the face kind of obvious). But regardless, the films always tried to say something, to go beyond the action and adventure. And because of this the franchise had broad appeal; to children and adults, to the intellectual and the average Joe.

However, Planet of the Apes' evolution themes and some of its depictions of religion have given some the impression that the film series has an anti-religious agenda. Having apes believe they were made in God's image (for instance) could be seen as a mocking of the similar Judeo-Christian belief that man was made in God's image. And Dr. Zaius couldn't be a more perfect stereotype of a "defender of the faith" who denies and opposes scientific discovery. The Sacred Scrolls (which

INTRODUCTION

have a very similar tone to the King James Bible), that is the basis of the apes' society and faith, turns out to be a fiction. There is definitely a satiricalness to the depictions of religion.

But, is that satiricalness a condemnation or just part of the upside down world of the Planet of the Apes? Moreover, does not the very inclusion of religion denote its importance in a society, whether it be man or ape?

While interpreting the films as attacking or demeaning religion is a valid interpretation, as a Christian I have never viewed the *Apes* films that way. In fact, I see many of the Christian values and teaching that I hold dear on display. I see parallels to biblical stories and figures. I see biblical truths shining through the science-fiction veneer.

Now obviously the creators of the Planet of the Apes series were not intending to proselytize the teachings of the Christian faith in what they called their "monkey movie." However, many of the racial and social commentaries in the films weren't intentional either. Some were, but others happened by accident as an outgrowth of the stories and characters, and the creative decisions in the filming—perhaps subconsciously. But intentional or otherwise, the films have powerful messages that have influenced their audiences.

In that vein, I believe that there are a number of messages in the *Apes* films that align with or support the moral and ethical teachings of the Christian Church. Some of these messages may not adhere to every denomination's beliefs; as there are many different sects of Christianity (each with their own dogma and biblical interpretations). However, in a general sense, these moral and ethical messages within the *Apes* films fit into the larger understanding of biblical teaching that Christians hold.

The analysis of each film will show distinct themes and messages in the plots and characters that advance or depict a Judeo-Christian philosophy. Some of these could be applied to multiple *Apes* films—as there are reappearing and continuing themes that run throughout all of the films. However, I believe that each film has something unique to say and is worthy of its own discussion. Even the remakes, while similar, emphasize different elements that in-turn affects what it's saying to the audience.

Now, I will willfully acknowledge that as a Christian I am predisposed to see the world through the value system that I was taught and came to believe in. Others may not see the *Apes* films the way that I do. And I am not so arrogant as to assert that my views on these films are definitive in any way, or are how they should be viewed by everyone, or that they were intended by the filmmakers. But that's one of the beautiful things about art—its ability to speak to different people in different ways, to open up a dialog and get people thinking and seeing things anew.

And ever since its initial release in 1968, *Planet of the Apes* (and its sequels) has spurred a discussion that continues to this day. And, as new audiences from different generations and cultural backgrounds are exposed to the series, the discussion is enriched with the new perspectives that they bring. As with any discussion, there are some points that are widely agreed upon and others that fail to reach a consensus. But uncon-

INTRODUCTION

ventional and challenging views are sometimes the most fun.

It is my hope that the analyses presented will add to this discussion. It is not my intention to diminish others' interpretations of these films or to deny the clear social commentaries that they make about prejudice, classism, and violence. I only wish to share some of what I see, as a person of faith, when I watch the *Apes* films; to bring to light issues and messages that you may not have considered before. Now, let me show you God on the Planet of the Apes.

> Jeremiah 29:13 – *You will seek me and find me when you seek me with all your heart.*

"It's a madhouse! A madhouse!"

CHAPTER 1: PLANET OF THE APES

Director: Franklin J. Schaffner
Screenplay: Michael Wilson and Rod Serling
Cast: Charlton Heston as Taylor
    Roddy McDowall as Cornelius
    Kim Hunter as Zira
    Maurice Evans as Dr. Zaius
    Linda Harrison as Nova

PLOT

While preparing to go into cryosleep with the rest of his crew, an astronaut named Taylor records one final entry into the ship's log confirming Dr. Hasslein's time relativity theory that while only 6 months have passed for the crew in space, nearly 700 years have passed back on Earth. When the ship makes an unexpected crash-landing into a lake the crew is awakened. The ship begins to flood and three of the four astronauts make it out; the fourth having died during cryosleep due to a malfunction. But before leaving they take what supplies they can and Taylor checks the Earth time recorder, which reads 3978–over 2,000 year have passed on Earth during their voyage.

When they get to shore they find that the land is inhospitable; there are strange lightning storms and no moon. After several days of trekking across deserts and mountains, they find a valley with primitive humans who are mute and are scavenging for food. But soon a

CHAPTER 1

group of hunters descends upon the valley—causing the humans to flee. The astronauts get swept up amongst the chaos and are separated. When Taylor sees the faces of his hunters he is horrified to discover that they are giant human sized apes wearing uniforms and carrying riffles. Before long he's herded into a trap along with several other humans and is shot in the throat, and when he's put into a carrel he's shocked to see that the apes can talk.

Sometime later Taylor finds himself in a cage with other humans having his wounds tended to by an ape doctor name Zira. After several failed attempts to communicate with her, Taylor steals her notepad and pencil and slips her a note with his name on it—demonstrating that he can write. She then brings him back to her office and he begins to explain that he's an astronaut from another world, which Zira shares with her finance Cornelius; an archeologist with unconventional views about the evolution of ape kind.

The Minister of Science, Dr. Zaius, starts to have suspicions about Taylor being different from the other humans when he visits Zira, and tries to have him moved. But before he can be taken, Taylor escapes and tries to get out of the city. However, he is captured once again, but with his wound healed he reveals that he can talk—shocking the assembled crowd around him.

A tribunal is assembled and Taylor once again tries to explain who he is and where he comes from. But things go badly, resulting in Taylor being put under the care of Dr. Zaius and Zira and Cornelius are charged with scientific heresy. To save Taylor and clear themselves of the charges against them, Zira and Cornelius arrange for Taylor's escape, along with a female companion named Nova that he's grown attached to, and takes them to the Forbidden Zone near where Taylor landed, hoping to find proof of their heretical claims in an abandoned archeological dig. When Zaius catches up to them he gives them a chance to prove their claims; which they are able to do with a talking human doll that Nova discovers. Taylor is then allowed to go off with Nova, and as they ride along the shoreline Taylor comes face-to-face with the ruins of the Statue of Liberty and realizes that he's been on Earth all along.

REVIEW

A cinematic classic, the original *Planet of the Apes* is one of the most influential and powerful films of the science-fiction genre. While Pierre Boulle considered it one of his lesser novels, in the hands of screenwriters Michael Wilson and Rod Serling it became a revolutionary film that continues to speak to audiences. Interestingly, Serling tried something similar several years earlier in *The Twilight Zone* episode "I Shot an Arrow into the Air."

The cast that producer Arthur P. Jacobs was able to assemble for this "monkey movie" is amazing: Charlton Heston, Roddy McDowall, Kim Hunter, Maurice Evans. Accomplished, respected actors. And they all give incredible performances that allow the audience to suspend disbelief and accept that these are talking ape people, and that they are real characters and not just makeup and masks. And the makeup too (which would earn a special Academy Award) is phenomenal. There is just something captivating about the designs.

CHAPTER 1

Much has been made about the political themes in the film; which address such issues as evolution, race, class, and the nature of violence. However, as is the case with the best science-fiction, there's a nuance to how the issues are presented. The film functions more as a dialog to get the viewers thinking rather than presenting a singular view. There are no answers. Taylor never learns what lead to the rise of apes, only that man destroyed himself in a nuclear war. And while Cornelius finds artifacts of an advanced human culture, there's nothing to support his theory that ape evolved from man.

But there is one thing that distinguishes the film more than any other, and that's the shocking twist ending: it was Earth the whole time. A change from the book that would become a defining part of the film series. Over fifty years later, it's a spoiled ending that everyone knows, and it has been parodied numerous times in other films and television shows (most notably on *The Simpsons*). Yet even knowing that it's coming, the imagery is extremely powerful and evocative. The juxtaposition of using the Statue of Liberty, a beacon of hope, as a symbol of death and destruction is a haunting visual that still resonates.

Planet of the Apes is a smart and daring film that ventures into the darkest reaches of the imagination. Some of it has dated, but most of it still holds up. We still face the same social and political issues that the film addresses. It still reflects our aspirations and our fears. And it set a strong foundation for future films to continue exploring the human condition and to push the boundaries of filmmaking.

THE DIVINE SPARK

The *Apes* series begins with a bang, tackling a lot of issues in its first outing. And one of its main themes is discovery; both figuratively and literary. First, the apes discover a talking, intelligent man in their mist—an unprecedented event that shocks their society to the core. And Taylor also discovers the unthinkable; talking apes and a humanity that has regressed to mute animals.

But more discoveries await as Dr. Zaius, Cornelius, and Zira have their convictions tested, and as Taylor confronts some hard truths about himself and the nature of man. And in these discoveries there are spiritual lessons that we can take away and apply to our Christian walk. For we too have discoveries to make in our lives and our relationships to God, each other, and the world around us.

HIDDEN KNOWLEDGE

Taylor mocks Dr. Zaius, calling him, "Defender of the Faith. Guardian of the Terrible Secret." But he actually is a guardian, protecting his people and society from a truth and a past that they are not ready for. As evidenced at Taylor's trial where the judges cover their eyes, ears, and mouths at the mere mention of a "missing link" in their evolution by Cornelius and Zira, ape society is not developed enough to accept intelligent humans—let alone a shared ancestry with them. Even common, working class apes such as Julius see Taylor as a freak.

Having been warned in the Sacred Scrolls about the destructiveness of man, "Beware the beast man, for he

CHAPTER 1

is the Devil's pawn. Alone among God's primates, he kills for sport or lust or greed. Yea, he will murder his brother to possess his brother's land," and knowing that his people aren't ready to face that breed of man, Dr. Zaius chooses to conceal any trace of intelligent humans. When Cornelius' archeological expedition into the Forbidden Zone gets too close to finding remnants of human civilization, Zaius has his permits revoked. And when he sees fragments of writing in a human cage, he scratches it out.

We too are a developing people who are not fully ready to know the things of God. Scripture reveals that God has placed limits on us throughout our journey from Eden to Babel to the modern today, and has kept things secret that are not for us to know; not out of malice but out of love as a caring Father looking out for His children as they grow.

- Genesis 2:17 – *[B]ut you must not eat from the tree of the knowledge of good and evil, for when you eat from it you will certainly die.*

- Deuteronomy 29:29 – *The secret things belong to the L*ORD *our God, but the things revealed belong to us and to our children forever, that we may follow all the words of this law.*

- 1 Corinthians 2:14 – *The person without the Spirit does not accept the things that come from the Spirit of God but considers them foolishness, and cannot understand them because they are discerned only through the Spirit.*

- 1 Corinthians 4:5 – *Therefore judge nothing before the appointed time; wait until the Lord comes. He will bring to light what is hidden in darkness and will expose the motives of the heart. At that time each will receive their praise from God.*

As Taylor rides along the beach and is confronted by the war-torn remnants of his long dead society in the decayed ruins of the Statue of Liberty, it becomes all too clear why Dr. Zaius has kept hidden the things of man. Unprepared to handle his technology, man rushed himself into an early graved; letting his wisdom "walk hand-in-hand with his idiocy." Wanting a different path for ape kind, the Lawgiver set out to conceal man's fate to allow ape society to develop free of man's past and its influences. And the result: a society without war or murder.

LIVE BY THE SWORD, DIE BY THE SWORD

In his last ship's log before going into cryosleep, Taylor asks if man "still make[s] war against his brother" and hopes that the descendants that are listening to his log are a better breed than the one he left. But despite his lofty soliloquy, Taylor is the man of violence that he condemns. After escaping from Ape City, the first thing he does is to arm himself despite Cornelius' assurance that they won't need guns. And when he takes Dr. Zaius hostage at the archeological dig, he threatens to kill him if his demands aren't met.

After being taken hostage, Dr. Zaius reveals that he has always known about man, and deemed him to be a "warlike creature who gives battle to everything around

CHAPTER 1

him, even himself." He also reveals that the Forbidden Zone was once a paradise that man turned into a desert. Upon leaving, Taylor tells Zaius not to follow him and boasts that he's "pretty handy" with a rifle, which Zaius fervently believes.

The Lord has warned us throughout Scripture that violence leads to a destructive path, one that we should not follow. For not only does it cause physical harm, but it corrupts the spirit and the mind.

- Psalm 11:5 – *The LORD examines the righteous, but the wicked, those who love violence, he hates with a passion.*

- Proverbs 3:31 – *Do not envy the violent or choose any of their ways.*

- Matthew 26:52 – *"Put your sword back in its place," Jesus said to him, "for all who draw the sword will die by the sword."*

- 1 Peter 3:9 – *Do not repay evil with evil or insult with insult. On the contrary, repay evil with blessing, because to this you were called so that you may inherit a blessing.*

While been held hostage, Dr. Zaius alludes to "evidence" that proves man's violent, destructive nature, and warns Taylor not to go looking for it; telling him, "You may not like what you find." But Taylor ignores him and rides off with Nova along the beach. Soon they come upon a decayed, rusting metal structure that is revealed to be the Stature of Liberty. Upon seeing this Taylor realizes that Zaius has been right all along; that man, in his thirst for violence, destroyed himself, and he cries out, "You maniacs! You blew it up. Oh, damn you. God damn you all to hell!"

TRUTHFUL WITNESS

After Taylor reveals his ability to talk during his failed attempt to escape the city, a tribunal is assembled. Rather than remain silent, Cornelius and Zira take up Taylor's defense. However, they are warned by the tribunal about the consequences of defending Taylor; telling them "that they endanger their own careers," and are given a chance to withdraw, but they stand by Taylor.

At first Cornelius and Zira only repeat the claims that Taylor has made about being an astronaut from another world who crash-landed and trekked through the mountains to reach the city, and argue semantics about whether a non-ape can have rights under Ape Law. But the obstinacy and injustice of the court soon compels them to stand up for Taylor; as Cornelius confirms everything Taylor has said about his journey (having also been to the Forbidden Zone), and Zira testifies to her belief in a "missing link in an evolutionary chain" that could explain Taylor's intelligence and ability to speak, and Cornelius supports her. After this, the prosecutor charges Cornelius and Zira with scientific heresy for speaking contrary to the Sacred Scrolls.

Scripture tells us that we are called to truthfulness in our affairs, no matter the cost, and to give witness to the Word of the Lord. And while this may be difficult at times, it is also freeing for the soul.

CHAPTER 1

- Proverbs 19:9 – *A false witness will not go unpunished, and whoever pours out lies will perish.*

- Acts 22:15 – *You will be his witness to all people of what you have seen and heard.*

- 1 Peter 3:15 – *[I]n your hearts revere Christ as Lord. Always be prepared to give an answer to everyone who asks you to give the reason for the hope that you have. But do this with gentleness and respect,*

- Ephesians 4:25 – *Therefore each of you must put off falsehood and speak truthfully to your neighbor, for we are all members of one body.*

Charged with scientific heresy, Cornelius and Zira flee to the Forbidden Zone with Taylor; intent on proving their theories and clearing their names. When Dr. Zaius catches up with them at Cornelius' archeological dig, he gives Cornelius a chance to prove his theories. But despite Cornelius' claims that "[s]ome of the evidence is uncontestable," Zaius remains unconvinced. That is, until Taylor presents him with a talking doll that Nova finds, and finally he can no longer deny the truth.

ALPHA AND OMEGA

The Christian walk is full of discovery. Reading the Word and growing in our relationship with God leads to an increasing knowledge of ourselves, the world, and of God. Yet there are things that are only for God to know, and part of trusting God is accepting this. He has a long-term plan that encompasses all of time and beyond. And to think that we could comprehend all of the secrets of the universe is foolish. As Albert Einstein once said, "The more I learn, the more I realize how much I don't know."

And while there are things that we don't know, we do know that our Lord wants the best for us, and He has commanded that we seek a path of nonviolence: to rise above our natural instincts to repay evil for evil and take retribution. It is often a struggle to cleanse ourselves of feelings of vengeance and hate, but satiating those feelings will only poison our souls and make it more difficult to know God and be in His presence.

Hate and anger will also damage our witness. We are called to be representatives of Christ and to proclaim the Good News. If we harbor ill will in our hearts and practice deceit, our light will not shine; the good work that God wants to do through us will go unfinished. To be effective in our ministry we must work to be like Christ; we must resist the anger and violence within us, we must be truthful in all things, and we must care for one another.

Discovery is a complicated process. We may find out that we are not who we think we are, that the people we thought we knew, we don't, that God is not who we thought He was. And we may come to doubt. But another part of trusting in God is to put away our doubts and to have faith. Faith that God is working all things for the good, that He is in control, that His Word is true and will see us through the trials and tribulations that lay before us, and that all will be revealed at its proper time.

CHAPTER 1

Luke 8:17 – *For there is nothing hidden that will not be disclosed, and nothing concealed that will not be known or brought out into the open.*

"I reveal my inmost self onto my God."

CHAPTER 2: BENEATH THE PLANET OF THE APES

Director: Ted Post
Screenplay: Paul Dehn
Cast: James Franciscus as Brent
   Kim Hunter as Zira
   Maurice Evans as Dr. Zaius
   Linda Harrison as Nova
   James Gregory as Gen. Ursus
   David Watson as Cornelius
   Charlton Heston as Taylor

PLOT

Brent, an astronaut on a rescue mission sent to find Col. Taylor after his ship was presumed lost, crashes in the Forbidden Zone where he finds Nova. Seeing that she's wearing Taylor's dog tags, he asks her to take him to Taylor. But instead Nova takes him to Ape City where a council of war is being held. Brent is shocked and horrified by the council; seeing talking apes and hearing cheers and applause at the rallying cry to invade the Forbidden Zone and to kill the humans there.

During the council Nova sees Cornelius and Zira, and takes Brent to them when the council ends. Cornelius and Zira are amazed to meet another human who can talk and agree to help him to find Taylor, and they give him new clothes to blend in and a map. However, Brent and Nova are captured by a patrol and are sent to be target practice for the soldiers. But Zira in-

CHAPTER 2

tercepts the wagon carrying them and unlocks the cage door; allowing Brent and Nova to escape and flee to an underground cavern.

In the cavern Brent recognizes familiar markings and realizes that it's the New York subway and that he's on Earth, and that some cataclysmic event must have upended the world he knew. A strange noise gets his attention and he and Nova follow it through the ruins of New York City until they reach a cathedral. Inside the cathedral a mutant with telepathic powers awaits, and Brent is taken away to be interrogated.

While Brent and Nova are held captive by the mutants, Dr. Zaius and an ape army under the command of Gen. Ursus march across the Forbidden Zone. The mutants attempt to stop the ape army with their mind powers, but are unsuccessful. Before long the apes breach the mutant city and begin destroying it, and gun down anyone they come across.

After being interrogated, Brent is taken to a prison cell where he finds Taylor held captive. They then team-up and breakout, but Nova is killed in the process. Fearing that the mutants will set off an Alpha-Omega atomic bomb that they worship, Taylor and Brent head for the cathedral. When they arrive they find that the apes have killed all of the mutants, and in an ensuing firefight Gen. Ursus and Brent are killed and Taylor is left mortally wounded. He asks for help from Dr. Zaius but is refused, and with his dying breath Taylor reaches out for the bomb control panel and activates it—destroy all life on the planet.

REVIEW

In many ways *Beneath the Planet of the Apes* is a predictable sequel that delivers more of the same: another astronaut out of the past crash-lands, has an adventure in Ape City, and makes the horrible discovery that the planet he's on is the Earth of the future. And it goes bigger with more chases, more fight scenes, and more ruined landmarks of New York City. But it also builds upon the original; answering the questions of why Dr. Zaius was so convinced that Taylor came from another "fort" within the Forbidden Zone and what was behind the strange phenomena that Taylor and his crew saw there.

Additionally, the great casting continues with James Franciscus, James Gregory, and Natalie Trundy. Gregory in particular gives an outstanding performance and sets the standard for future gorilla generals in the series. Also, Linda Harrison steps up her game and gives a nuanced performance that shows her character's continuing development. And Charlton Heston has a powerful death scene that's a real highlight of the film.

What is not so impressive though, are the cheap ape masks used for the background characters. And the ruins of New York City are rather lackluster; having none of the impact that the Statue of Liberty had in the first film. Furthermore, the scenes in which Brent realizes that he's on Earth are underwhelming to the say the least—illustrating some of the weaknesses in the script.

Yet the hook for the film, the mutants, proves to be remarkably compelling. While corners were cut with the ape masks, the mutant masks are grotesquely real-

CHAPTER 2

istic. The scene in the cathedral where the mutants reveal their true faces is incredibly disturbing—nightmarish—and a testament to the skill of makeup artist John Chambers (who's still bringing his A-game). And the addition of the mutants enriches the mythos of the series—raising all kinds of fascinating questions.

Beneath the Planet of the Apes is a lesser film than the original; as the writing, directing, and artistry aren't at the same level. But as sequels go, it's a solid follow-up that honors the provocative nature of the material; which continues to explore sociopolitical issues and science-fiction concepts. In fact, it's rather surprising how well the film's able to shift directions to explore new issues. The execution may be a little lacking, but there's much to appreciate in this second installment.

THE DIVINE SPARK

Of all the films in the series, *Beneath the Planet of the Apes* is the one that most explicitly deals with religion. The apes embark on a holy war (a crusade if you will) to retake the Forbidden Zone. But the endeavor will not be easy. They will have their faith tested. They will see and experience things that will cause them to doubt their beliefs.

But it's not just the apes who are tested. The mutants in the Forbidden Zone, descendants of humanity, will also face trails. With the apes on the war path, their commitment to peace and non-violence will be tested. Their fundamental religious belief in the Alpha-Omega bomb as a "holy weapon of peace" will be tested. A number of religious themes play out in this war story, and we can learn much from it.

CHURCH FELLOWSHIP

Before embarking on their quest into the Forbidden Zone, the ape army gathers for a religious service. An ape priest gives a blessing to the soldiers assuring them of the righteousness of their cause and requests divine protection: "O God, bless, we pray you, our great army and its supreme commander on the eve of a holy war undertaken for your sake." Gen. Ursus, Dr. Zaius, and the soldiers kneel and pray with the priest; affirming their devotion to their god and their unity as a community.

The mutants too hold a prayer service. The mutant leader, Mendez, and the council gather their people together in their cathedral to sing songs of praise and worship to their creator and to be in his presence. They also welcome Brent and Nova to join their service, sharing their faith and fellowship with them, hoping to convince them of their "peaceful intentions."

The Scriptures tell us that we in Christ are a body, and must fellowship together to nurture and to grow. For we need each other for encouragement, worship, and prayer; for it is only together that we can realize our potential and fulfil our purpose as Christ's church.

- Acts 2:42 – *They devoted themselves to the apostles' teaching and to fellowship, to the breaking of bread and to prayer.*

- Romans 12:4-5 – *For just as each of us has one body with many members, and these members do not all have the same function, so in Christ*

CHAPTER 2

we, though many, form one body, and each member belongs to all the others.

- Colossians 3:16 – *Let the message of Christ dwell among you richly as you teach and admonish one another with all wisdom through psalms, hymns, and songs from the Spirit, singing to God with gratitude in your hearts.*

- 1 John 1:7 – *[I]f we walk in the light, as he is in the light, we have fellowship with one another, and the blood of Jesus, his Son, purifies us from all sin.*

Ironically, the final confrontation between the mutants and apes takes place in the mutant's cathedral. Perhaps hoping that a house of faith would weaken the spirit of war that has hold over the apes, Mendez chooses the cathedral as the place to make his last pleas for peace. He also shares his god's glory in the vestige of the Alpha-Omega bomb, which he raises from its housing. But Gen. Ursus is unmoved and Mendez is martyred for his faith when he's gunned down.

CONFRONT HERESY

The mutants make a critical mistake in their attack on the ape army; they follow their illusion of fields of crucified apes with an image of a giant statue of the Lawgiver bleeding. The image shocks and appalls the apes. A bleeding Lawgiver contradicts their beliefs and causes them to doubt. Gen. Ursus is frozen, unsure of what to do, until Dr. Zaius proclaims that it's "a vision, and it is a lie" and rides out to confront it. Seeing this, the mutants then try to scare off Zaius by having the statue fall on him. But Zaius holds his ground and his example gives the apes courage; leading them to continue their march into the Forbidden Zone.

When they enter the mutant's city, the apes are again confronted with heretical images. As they walk through the halls they see graven images glorifying man. Again Dr. Zaius takes action; he calls them "obscene" and destroys them. Seeing his example, the ape soldiers also knockdown the statues that adorn the city halls.

Similarly, Scripture commanded us to hold true to the teachings of the Lord and to confront those who twist the Word of God and lead His people astray. Heresy is always waiting to pop-up should we grow complacent and fail to weed it out.

- Galatians 1:9 – *As we have already said, so now I say again: If anybody is preaching to you a gospel other than what you accepted, let them be under God's curse!*

- 2 Thessalonians 2:15 – *[B]rothers and sisters, stand firm and hold fast to the teachings we passed on to you, whether by word of mouth or by letter.*

- Titus 1:9 – *He must hold firmly to the trustworthy message as it has been taught, so that he can encourage others by sound doctrine and refute those who oppose it.*

- 2 Peter 2:1 – *But there were also false prophets among the people, just as there will be false teachers among you. They will secretly introduce destructive heresies, even denying the*

CHAPTER 2

sovereign Lord who bought them—bringing swift destruction on themselves.

In their final confrontation with the mutants, Mendez tells the apes to behold "the instrument of [his] god," and raise the Alpha-Omega bomb from its housing. However, Gen. Ursus isn't deterred by this demonstration and shoots at it. Determined to expose and destroy this false idol, Ursus commands his soldiers to tear down the Alpha-Omega bomb.

POSSESSION

The mutants in the Forbidden Zone have telepathic powers that allow them to possess a person's mind and control them. They begin by making Brent hear sounds that aren't there in order to lead him to their cathedral. They also force him to choke Nova against his will—nearly killing her. And when he tries to resist their interrogation about his knowledge of Ape City, they inflict pain throughout his body until he crumbles to the floor.

The apes too have their minds invaded by the mutants; causing them to see a field of apes crucified upside down burning in a raging fire. So real are these images in their minds, that the soldiers begin crying out and jumping in furious anger. Even Dr. Zaius is convinced by the mutant's mind invasion, and he pleads with Gen. Ursus to order his men to shoot the burning apes to save them from a painful death in the fires: "If you have any pity, bid your soldiers to shoot our poor people."

The Scriptures are replete with people being possessed and controlled by spirits who do harm to their vessels and change them. And while it may not seem as common place today, it is something the faithful should be aware of and prepared to confront.

- Matthew 8:16 – *When evening came, many who were demon-possessed were brought to [Jesus], and he drove out the spirits with a word and healed all the sick.*

- Luke 9:38-39 – *A man in the crowd called out, "Teacher, I beg you to look at my son, for he is my only child. A spirit seizes him and he suddenly screams; it throws him into convulsions so that he foams at the mouth. It scarcely ever leaves him and is destroying him."*

- Luke 11:14 – *Jesus was driving out a demon that was mute. When the demon left, the man who had been mute spoke, and the crowd was amazed.*

- Acts 16:18 – *Finally Paul became so annoyed that he turned around and said to the spirit, "In the name of Jesus Christ I command you to come out of her!" At that moment the spirit left her.*

The full extent of the mutants' abilities to possess the mind comes when Brent is locked in a cell with Taylor, and one of the mutants puppeteers them in a fight to the death. He unlocks the cell door and throws in a mace, then uses his powers to make Brent and Taylor fight. And while they try to resist, the mutant's powers are too strong, and they deliver blow after blow, bloodying each other up until Nova distracts the mutant—breaking his control over them. Freed of the mutant's control, Brent and Taylor then work together to overpower and kill the mutant and break out of their cell.

ALPHA AND OMEGA

Our faith in Christ will be tested in both good times and in bad. And we will not always pass. Even Peter the Apostle, the rock Christ built His Church on, denied Him. But the Good News is that there is redemption and forgiveness in Christ. The question is, will we seek the redemption and forgiveness that He offers? Will we move forward? Will we learn and grow from our failures?

As John Donne once wrote, "No man is an island." If we are to succeed in our walk of faith we will need church fellowship to strength us, to guide us, and to support us. We all have different needs and different gifts, and the Church helps us to complete ourselves and to fulfill our purpose: to serve and worship the Lord. God doesn't want us to be lone warriors fighting the good fight alone. He wants us to be a body with each part working in tandem to accomplish great things.

Yet the closer we get to the spiritual, the more susceptible we become to spiritual attack. Scripture tells us that we are in a war "against the spiritual forces of evil in the heavenly realms" (Ephesians 6:12). So it is incumbent on us to protect our mind, body, and spirit through prayer and communion with the Lord and His Church.

Holding true to the faith is not always easy. Deceivers will come to challenge us and will attempt to lead us astray. And at times they may succeed and cause us to falter. Yet as long we continue to strive to be more like Christ, as long as we work towards living out the Gospel, we will overcome the trials and tribulations before us. For the test of our faith is not whether we have sinned, but whether we have the blood of the Lamb.

> 2 Timothy 4:7 – *I have fought the good fight, I have finished the race, I have kept the faith.*

"We came from your future."

CHAPTER 3: ESCAPE FROM THE PLANET OF THE APES

Director: Don Taylor
Screenplay: Paul Dehn
Cast: Roddy McDowall as Cornelius
 Kim Hunter as Zira
 Bradford Dillman as Dr. Lewis Dixon
 Natalie Trundy as Dr. Stephanie Branton
 Eric Braeden as Dr. Otto Hasslein
 Ricardo Montalbán as Armando

PLOT

Off the coast of California, the U.S. military recovers the spacecraft that was led by Col. Taylor and was presumed lost along with its crew. Upon opening the craft, it's discovered that there are three occupants aboard. But they are not Col. Taylor and his crew. When unmasked, it is revealed that they are apes: Cornelius, Zira, and Milo. Milo, a mechanical genius, was able to recover the ship in 3955 and took it on a test flight with Cornelius and Zira, but was caught in the shockwaves from the detonation of the Alpha-Omega atomic bomb and sent back in time to 1973.

The apes are taken to the Los Angeles Zoo and examined by Drs. Dixon and Branton to discover how they came into possession of the ship and learned to operate it. When an accident occurs at the zoo in which

Milo is killed, Cornelius and Zira take Dixon and Branton into their confidence; revealing that they can speak and are from a highly evolved society where apes speak and humans are dumb. However, it isn't until they appear before an investigative committee that they share Dr. Milo's theory that they are from Earth's future and were thrown into the past.

Following their testimony before the committee, Cornelius and Zira are freed from the Los Angeles Zoo and are given a hotel suite. Before long they become celebrities and are taken on shopping sprees and given tours of museums. But things change when the President's science advisor, Dr. Otto Hasslein, discovers that Zira is pregnant and coaches a confession from her that she witnessed the Earth destroyed before they traveled back in time.

Armed with this new evidence that Cornelius and Zira have held back information from the committee, Hasslein has them detained at a military base and subjected to intense interrogation. Fearing for their safety, Cornelius and Zira escape the base and seek help from Dixon and Branton; who arrange for them to be given shelter at Armando's Circus where Zira gives birth to a son.

Meanwhile, Hasslein leads a search to find Cornelius and Zira; which forces them to leave the circus and head for a shipyard full of derelict vessels to hide in. However, Hasslein eventual tracks them to the shipyard, and in a standoff with the police Hasslein, Cornelius, Zira, and their baby are all killed. But secretly, Zira (fearing the worst) had switched her baby with another at Armando's Circus before they left, and as Armando packs up his circus tent and prepares to move on Cornelius and Zira's baby says his first word, "Mama."

REVIEW

While it's one of the weaker entries in the franchise, *Escape from the Planet of the Apes* deserves recognition for its creativity and almost seamless ability to continue the over-arcing story. Many sequels are jarring from one entry to the next, with few (if any) connecting strands. But here, having Cornelius and Zira, the newly appointed ministers of science in Dr. Zaius' absence, testing Taylor's recovered spaceship and being impacted by the detonation of the Alpha-Omega bomb, is a fairly smooth transition into a new adventure.

Also, the switch to a more comedic tone is a daring decision that works and allows the series to have a little fun with Cornelius and Zira being fish-out-of-water; having to adapt to a world run by humans. Yet the film doesn't stay there. Wisely, it doesn't let the comedy wear out its welcome and segues into political drama and chases in the second half.

Roddy McDowall returns to the series to join Kim Hunter and they give it their all, and are able to sell both the comedy and the drama. Also returning is Natalie Trundy, who is given a nice showcase as an empathetic scientist who helps Cornelius and Zira (and Trundy will appear throughout the rest of the original series in different roles). And Ricardo Montalbán brings a fun energy as an eccentric circus owner.

One of the strongest criticisms of the film are the numerous continuity errors; as screenwriter Paul Dehn seems to be setting up a new mythology. Although, there have been several comics and novels that have provided explanations for these inconsistencies (to varying degrees of success) for those who want them. Nevertheless, the apparent changes in the series mythology aren't so egregious so as to ruin the story. As was the case with the last film, the greatest weaknesses stem from the budget cuts; which result in some very poor ape costumes and a couple of cheap looking sets.

Escape from the Planet of the Apes gives the series a new energy and allows for the continued exploration of sociopolitical issues from a new perspective. And as with the previous films, it's not afraid to take risks and to go in unexpected directions. Some audiences may have problems adjusting to this new direction; but for those who can, a rewarding and thought-provoking experience awaits.

THE DIVINE SPARK

Escape from the Planet of the Apes explores the nature of prophecy. Cornelius and Zira travel from Earth's future to its past, and bring an apocalyptic prophecy of doom—giving humanity a glimpse of what is to come. And how the characters react is telling; Dr. Otto Hasslein, a man of science, choices to fight the future, while Armando, a man of faith, accepts it without reservation. The course of the future is at stake, but can it be controlled or altered?

Hasslein believes that there are multiple futures that can be picked from. But are Hasslein, Cornelius, and Zira choosing a future with their actions or following a destiny that has already been determined by God (as Armando believes)? It's a question that fans of the se-

CHAPTER 3

ries have often debated. Did Cornelius and Zira's traveling to the past alter history, or was it completing a loop? This and many other issues are presented in this third entry into the *Apes* franchise.

USE YOUR TALENTS

When the apes are brought to the Los Angeles Zoo they are very careful about revealing their ability to speak to their human captors; as Milo warns Cornelius and Zira that "there is a time for truth, and a time, not for lies, but for silence." They change into their native clothes and use utensils to eat their food, but they do not speak–or demonstrate any other ability to communicate. But this changes when Drs. Dixon and Branton start administering tests. After completing a geometric puzzle to build a stair to receive a banana, Dr. Branton asks, "Why doesn't she take it?" To which Zira replies, "Because I loathe bananas!"

With their secret out in the open, Cornelius and Zira begin talking to Dixon and Branton; who attempt to console them when Milo is killed by a gorilla in an adjoining cage. Dixon and Branton then prepare Cornelius and Zira for a presidential inquiry that is looking into what happened to astronaut Col. Taylor and how Cornelius and Zira ended up with his ship. At first the committee thinks that the apes are mimicking, but as the questioning continues Cornelius and Zira demonstrate their ability to think and to reason.

God has told us that we too are to use the talents that He has given us, and not to keep them hidden or to let them go to waste. We are all given talents of varying kinds and are commanded to use them for His glory.

- Matthew 5:14-16 – *You are the light of the world. A town built on a hill cannot be hidden. Neither do people light a lamp and put it under a bowl. Instead they put it on its stand, and it gives light to everyone in the house. In the same way, let your light shine before others, that they may see your good deeds and glorify your Father in heaven.*

- 1 Corinthians 7:7 – *I wish that all of you were as I am. But each of you has your own gift from God; one has this gift, another has that.*

- 2 Timothy 1:6 – *[F]an into flame the gift of God, which is in you*

- 1 Peter 4:10 – *Each of you should use whatever gift you have received to serve others, as faithful stewards of God's grace in its various forms.*

Following their testimony at the presidential inquiry, Cornelius and Zira are released from their cage at the zoo and are given a suite at a hotel. They also start utilizing their abilities more; as Zira is invited to be a guest lecturer at a women's club and Cornelius is asked to dedicate an amusement park ride at Disneyland. Additionally, they host a social gathering at their hotel and provide interviews with journalists about various topics.

OMNIPRESENCE

During the presidential inquiry, Zira reveals that she and Cornelius are from Earth's future. The commission members are shocked and view the idea as "preposterous." But for one member, Dr. Otto Hasslein, the revelation starts to make things clearer. In fact, he states that Zira's time travel theory is "the only explanation."

Later, while giving an interview with a news anchor, Dr. Hasslein confirms that Cornelius and Zira coming from the future is most likely true. He further states that "time can only be fully understood by an observer with a godlike gift of infinite regression"—the moment when one becomes "both the observer and the observed." Using a multilane freeway as an illustration, Hasslein explains that futures can be changed by moving from lane to lane and that time is malleable.

The Scriptures reveal that the Lord is both part of time and outside of it, without beginning or end, and moves through it unbound by our conception of time and space.

- Psalm 90:2 – *Before the mountains were born or you brought forth the whole world, from everlasting to everlasting you are God.*

- John 1:1-2 – *In the beginning was the Word, and the Word was with God, and the Word was God. He was with God in the beginning.*

- Hebrews 13:8 – *Jesus Christ is the same yesterday and today and forever.*

- 2 Peter 3:8 – *But do not forget this one thing, dear friends: With the Lord a day is like a thousand years, and a thousand years are like a day.*

When Dr. Hasslein takes his concerns about the future that Cornelius and Zira have described to the President, he wonders if the future can be changed:

"How many futures are there? And which future has God, if there is a God, chosen for man's destiny?" Similarly, Armando tells Cornelius and Zira that destiny is unalterable and is in God's hands.

THE END OF THE WORLD

"We think we've got all the time in the world! How much time has the world got?!" Following Zira's revelation of seeing "bright, white, blinding light" and "the rim of the Earth melt" during her space flight, Dr. Hasslein becomes obsessed with saving the world by stopping the rise of apes. At first he seeks permission from the President to have Cornelius and Zira questioned again by professionals. During this new questioning Cornelius tells Hasslein of the secret history that he had access to as a historian and when he and Zira were appointed temporary heads of the Ministry of Science, of a disease that wiped out cats and dogs, and of how apes were trained to replace them as pets.

However, learning of future events to avert in order to stop apes from rising to dominance isn't enough. Hasslein also seeks to abort Zira's unborn child and to prevent her and Cornelius from being able to conceive another. Believing intelligent apes to be a threat to the future of humanity and the safety of the world, Hasslein pushes to have Cornelius and Zira killed.

Throughout Scripture we are told that the world will come to an end; that it has already been ordained by the Father and is beyond our ability to predict or impede.

- Matthew 24:35-36 – *Heaven and earth will pass away, but my words will never pass away. But about that day or hour no one knows, not even the angels in heaven, nor the Son, but only the Father.*

- 1 Peter 4:7 – *The end of all things is near. Therefore be alert and of sober mind so that you may pray.*

- 2 Peter 3:10 – *But the day of the Lord will come like a thief. The heavens will disappear with a roar; the elements will be destroyed by fire, and the earth and everything done in it will be laid bare.*

- Revelation 21: 1 – *Then I saw "a new heaven and a new earth," for the first heaven and the first earth had passed away, and there was no longer any sea.*

Dr. Hasslein eventually takes it upon himself to save the world by personally hunting Cornelius and Zira down after discovering them hiding out on a derelict ship. He demands that Zira give up her child and shots her in the back when she refuses, and then proceeds to shoot the baby ape that she was carrying. Having eliminated mother and child, Hasslein believes that he has prevented the raise of intelligent apes and saved the world from the nuclear war that they unleash in 3955. But unknown to him, nothing has been stopped; for Zira had switched babies with Heloise at Armando's Circus, and the intelligent ape he feared would bring about the rise of the apes is safe and free to fulfill his destiny.

ALPHA AND OMEGA

The nature of God is still something that perplexed many believers. Having only our own finite existence to go off of, how do we conceive of a being without beginning or end, to which time has no meaning? It's a daunting concept to get one's head around...if one can. Like many things, it's something that, perhaps, cannot be fully understood and makes God the awe inspiring being that He is.

And it is because of His nature that God is able to give order to time and prophesy what is to come. We all know that He created the world, but we often forget that He has also set about its destruction. The end times are not an unknown destination that we are aimlessly moving toward. Many times throughout Scripture the Lord and His prophets have given prophecy to what will happen when the end is nigh. Not to scare us, but rather the opposite. To prepare us so that we are not given to panic and fear.

Without fear we are free to use our talents unabashedly and to proclaim the Word boldly. Knowing that the time we, and in deed the world, have is finite helps to give it and us purpose. Benjamin Franklin once said, "Don't put off until tomorrow what you can do today." And knowing that time is fleeting and that the world will pass away pushes us to do just that.

With the world's end already prophesied by God, the only question remaining is how will we react? Will we fight it like Hasslein and look for ways to craft a different future, or will we accept it and use that knowledge to make the best of the time that we have been given? Will we humble ourselves and use that strength to let

CHAPTER 3

our talents shine? Or will we resist God's will and waste what has been given to us?

> Psalm 39:5 – *You have made my days a mere handbreadth; the span of my years is as nothing before you. Everyone is but a breath, even those who seem secure.*

"Tonight we have seen the birth of the planet of the apes!"

CHAPTER 4: CONQUEST OF THE PLANET OF THE APES

Director: J. Lee Thompson
Screenplay: Paul Dehn
Cast: Roddy McDowall as Caesar
    Don Murray as Governor Breck
    Natalie Trundy as Lisa
    Hari Rhodes as MacDonald
    Severn Darden as Chief Inspector Kolp
    Ricardo Montalbán as Armando

PLOT

In a dystopian future a virus has wiped out cats and dogs, pathing the way for apes to be domesticated and turned into a servant caste that does menial labor for their human masters. Unaware of this, Caesar, the child of two talking apes from the distant future (Cornelius and Zira), is shocked and horrified when he sees apes being abused as he walks through a metropolitan city handing out fliers for his adopted father's circus.

    Armando, Caesar's adopted father, has kept Caesar safe at his circus for the past 20 years (ever since Caesar's parents were murdered) and has raised Caesar as his own. And when Caesar cries out upon seeing an ape being beaten by the police, Armando tries to cover for him and is taken into custody for questioning. Mean-

CHAPTER 4

while, Caesar is forced to hide among his own kind and is sold to the governor and trained to be a file worker.

Despite Armando's pleas of innocence, Chief Inspector Kolp suspects that he's lying to cover for his ape; who witnesses claim spoke. Upon further investigation, Kolp discovers that Armando's circus had an ape birth around the same time that the future apes had their child. Kolp then subjects Armando to intense interrogation and he begins to break. However, Armando is able to escape from his confines and throws himself out of a window and falls to his death.

Upon learning of Armando's death, Caesar begins plotting an ape rebellion. He starts to stockpile weapons and organizes the apes to be in key positions when the moment is right. But Chief Inspector Kolp is able to track Caesar down and captures him before Caesar can launch his revolt. Caesar is then tortured until he reveals that he is indeed the talking ape that they've been looking for. With his identity confirmed, Governor Breck orders Caesar's execution.

Feeling pity for Caesar, Governor Breck's aid, MacDonald, helps Caesar fake his death. Caesar then escapes and launches his rebellion—leading an ape army into the streets. A violent clash with the police erupts, but the apes are able to overpower them. The apes then march to Ape Management and free their brethren, and finally descend on the government center and capture Governor Breck. Caesar claims victory, but tells his soldiers to end the bloodshed and to retreat into the shadows where they will bide their time until man inevitably destroys himself.

REVIEW

One of the best entries in the series, *Conquest of the Planet of the Apes* is incredibly daring and pushes boundaries—going darker and more violent than ever before. It's a bit of a course correction from the last film; as there are few jokes or lighthearted moments. Rather, the film tackles some very serious issues, and it's reflected in the tone. To wit, the film had to undergo extensive editing to avoid an R rating.

Re-envisioning the dystopian future has come to be an essential part of *Apes* films (none of the original series films take place in their year of release), and the filmmakers have created a frighteningly, all too real, not too distant future. Obviously 1991 didn't exactly turn out as the film depicts, but it's not far off in its vision of a brutal police state (which America has steadily been moving towards). Increasing executive power and militarizing the police have come to pass, as has the power of the state to hold and detain persons without counsel.

Once again the cast rises to the occasion. Roddy McDowall gives an extraordinary performance and does an impressive job at distinguishing his new character of Caesar from that of his previous one. And Don Murray is especially good as well; creating a terrifically evil villain that has some complexity to him. Also, Ricardo Montalbán delivers a strong performance; taking on a more dramatic role than in the last film.

However, the continuity with the other films is problematic; as Cornelius and Zira described quite a different series of events that lead to the rise of apes than what we get here (though alternate timelines can be used to explain away such things). And just overall, the dystopic future of *Conquest* is a big leap from how things were left in the last film. Also, the ape makeup effects aren't good enough for the scale that the filmmakers are going for. Still, director J. Lee Thompson does an impressive job at hiding some of the film's limitations through efficacious use of the camera and other techniques.

Ultimately, like the first film, *Conquest of the Planet of the Apes* lives and dies on the ending, and it is one of the most visceral and evocative sequences in the entire series. Modeled after the real-life Watts riots, Caesar's rebellion is both riveting and terrifying. And far from becoming stale, the themes and issues that the series has explored are just as topical and thought-provoking in this installment as in the previous ones (if not more so). A smart and engaging thriller, *Conquest of the Planet of the Apes* is deserving of the praise that it receives.

THE DIVINE SPARK

Conquest of the Planet of the Apes is probably the least subtle *Apes* film and is pretty blatant in its antislavery message. Like the biblical forefather Joseph, Caesar is put into slavery and goes through trials that prepare him for the call of leadership. But what kind of leader will he be? One who seeks retribution or one who shows compassion?

Slavery comes in many forms, and as Governor Breck says, we have all been slaves "in one sense of the word or another." But will that blind us to slavery when we see it, like Breck, or lead us to be more sensitive to it, like MacDonald. We may not like to admit it, but slavery is all around us; in our mindsets, in our behaviors, in our addictions, our debts, in the limitations society (and we ourselves) place on us. And thus the film's themes are still relevant.

SACRIFICE

While touring the city, Caesar sees a group of police officers beating an ape and cries out, "Lousy human bastards!" Armando tries to cover for him and tells the police that he was the one who said it and takes responsibility. But in the commotion Caesar runs off before Armando can convince the police officers. To protect Caesar, Armando turns himself into the authorities hoping to explain away the incident and deflect any suspicion that Caesar spoke and is the child of Cornelius and Zira.

Armando is taken to Governor Breck and Chief Inspector Kolp and is interrogated about the incident with the police, and again he attempts to claim that it was he who yelled and that as a circus owner he has a certain empathy for animals. However, they are unconvinced and Kolp starts digging into Armando's past and discovers that a baby chimpanzee was born in his circus around the time Cornelius and Zira had their child.

We are told in the Scriptures that sacrificing oneself for another is one of the purest acts of love. It was modeled by our Lord, and we are to follow His example.

- John 10:11 – *I am the good shepherd. The good shepherd lays down his life for the sheep.*

CHAPTER 4

- John 15:13 – *Greater love has no one than this: to lay down one's life for one's friends.*

- Romans 5:8 – *God demonstrates his own love for us in this: While we were still sinners, Christ died for us.*

- 1 John 3:16 – *This is how we know what love is: Jesus Christ laid down his life for us. And we ought to lay down our lives for our brothers and sisters.*

After days of interrogation, Kolp brings in a device that forces a person to tell the truth. Armando tries to resist but finds himself revealing the secrets that he's been trying to keep. Knowing that he will be forced to give up Caesar and that Kolp will likely kill him when he finds him, Armando breaks free of his restraints and runs for a glass window. To protect Caesar's life, Armando chooses to sacrifice his own; throwing himself through the window and falling to his death.

FREEDOM

When Caesar visits the city with Armando, he is shocked to see that apes have been enslaved and are not mere pets—as he had been let to believe. And when Armando is held by the authorities, Caesar is forced to become a slave himself in order to avoid being discovered. Before long he is sold to Governor Breck and trained for file work. But try as he might, glimpses of Caesar's true nature show through his guise as he performs his tasks with little training and shows an awareness when he's told to pick a name out of a book.

Upon learning of Armando's death, Caesar faces a moment of crisis and decides that he must fight to regain his freedom by leading a revolution. He begins organizing the apes and holding secret meeting. Sensing there is something special about Caesar, the apes are drawn to him and look to him for leadership; realizing Governor Breck's fears that the apes have been "waiting for an ape with enough intelligence, with enough will to lead them...Waiting for an ape who can think, who can talk."

The Scriptures call us to live as free men and women, and to not let ourselves be shackled by sin or imprisoned by fear. Christ came to liberate us from all that keeps us from being in His glory.

- Isaiah 61:1 – *The Spirit of the Sovereign LORD is on me, because the LORD has anointed me to proclaim good news to the poor. He has sent me to bind up the brokenhearted, to proclaim freedom for the captives and release from darkness for the prisoners,*
- Galatians 5:1 – *It is for freedom that Christ has set us free. Stand firm, then, and do not let yourselves be burdened again by a yoke of slavery.*
- Galatians 5:13 – *You, my brothers and sisters, were called to be free. But do not use your freedom to indulge the flesh; rather, serve one another humbly in love.*
- 1 Peter 2:16 – *Live as free people, but do not use your freedom as a cover-up for evil; live as God's slaves.*

Things finally come to a head when Caesar narrowly escapes being killed by Governor Breck after he is discovered. Caesar then assembles his army to march on

CHAPTER 4

Ape Management to free their brethren. Breck puts the city on lockdown and calls out a riot squad to put down the rebelling apes. But they are soon overrun. The rebelling apes free their kin at Ape Management and then head for Breck's command center and force his surrender. Then Caesar tells the apes that they will go off on their own to live free and wait "for the inevitable day of man's downfall."

TURN THE OTHER CHEEK

As Caesar and his army attempt to force their way into Governor Breck's command center, Breck has his guards summarily execute the worker apes who are still there. However, Caesar breaches the center before they are all killed and manages to rescue an ape named Lisa. Breck is taken captive and brought out to the public square for judgment.

Amidst the rabble, the governor's aid, MacDonald, calls out to Caesar and pleads for mercy: "Caesar, I, a descendant of slaves, am asking you to show humanity!" But Caesar is too consumed by his own power and tells McDonald that his revolution will spread across the continents. He then signals the apes guarding Breck to kill him. Seeing the carnage and destruction around her, Lisa turns to Caesar and says, "No."

The Lord has repeatedly told us throughout Scripture that revenge is His and His alone, and we are not to repay evil for evil. For we are to be examples of God's love.

- Leviticus 19:18 – *Do not seek revenge or bear a grudge against anyone among your people,*

> but love your neighbor as yourself. I am the LORD.

- Luke 6:29 – *If someone slaps you on one cheek, turn to them the other also. If someone takes your coat, do not withhold your shirt from them.*

- Romans 12:19 – *Do not take revenge, my dear friends, but leave room for God's wrath, for it is written: "It is mine to avenge; I will repay," says the Lord.*

- Ephesians 4:32 – *Be kind and compassionate to one another, forgiving each other, just as in Christ God forgave you.*

Upon hearing Lisa's "No," Caesar has a change of heart and tells his army, "Now we will put away our hatred. Now we will put down our weapons...we, who are not human, can afford to be humane. Destiny is the will of God, and if it is man's destiny to be dominated, it is God's will that he be dominated with compassion and understanding. So, cast out your vengeance." And the apes then lower their weapons and allow Breck to live.

ALPHA AND OMEGA

Author Chuck Palahniuk once wrote, "The things you own end up owning you." Many people find themselves indentured to mortgages and loans, while others find themselves trapped by unhealthy behavior patterns and addictions. We are not the free men and women that God wants us to be. Without realizing it, we shackle ourselves rather than live the liberated lives He wants for us.

The Lord wants us to put others first and to sacrifice ourselves for one another. And in this way our material attachments and shackles grow weaker, and our bond of community grows stronger. It is also how we show love to our brethren and obedience to the Lord. As Christ demonstrated throughout His ministry, service to God begins with serving others.

The Lord also wants us to be free of the bindings that holding on to hatred and anger bring. Holding on to hate and anger prevents us from fully experiencing the love and joy that is all around us. And so he has commanded us not to take vengeance or repay evil for evil, but to let it go and forgive. By this we free ourselves of the negativity that keeps us down and clouds our lives.

Freedom is something that must constantly be fought for, for there are always those ready to take it from us should we give them the opportunity. To follow Christ we must let go of the things that bind us in whatever forms they may take: material attachments, legalism, vanity. But it doesn't stop there, for we must also help to liberate our fellow man so that they too can know the life God offers them and the joy it brings.

> 2 Corinthians 3:17 – *Now the Lord is the Spirit, and where the Spirit of the Lord is, there is freedom.*

"Ape shall never kill ape."

CHAPTER 5: BATTLE FOR THE PLANET OF THE APES

Director: J. Lee Thompson
Screenplay: John William Corrington & Joyce Hooper Corrington
Cast: Roddy McDowall as Caesar
  Claude Akins as General Aldo
  Natalie Trundy as Lisa
  Severn Darden as Governor Kolp
  Austin Stoker as MacDonald
  Paul Williams as Virgil

PLOT

Following a nuclear war, Caesar establishes a new community where apes and humans live together in peace. However, they are not equal and old resentments and prejudices still remain. Upon learning of government tapes of his parents that could shed light on what the future holds, Caesar mounts an expedition to go into the remains of a nearby city that was destroyed by an atomic bomb, known as the Forbidden City, to look for the tapes.

While exploring the remains of the city, Caesar and his team find the tapes and learn of the Earth's destruction in the future. They also discover that there are mutated humans living in the city, and narrowly escape capture. Upon learning of Caesar, Governor Kolp, the leader of the mutated humans, sends a scouting party after him to discover where he came from.

The scouts report back and the mutated humans assemble their army and prepare to march to the ape city and attack. However, a more dangerous threat looms for Caesar; as his military general, Aldo, secretly plots with his soldiers to kill Caesar and assume power by stealing guns from the armory. Aldo's plot is overheard by Caesar's son Cornelius, who chased his pet squirrel into a tree. Upon seeing Cornelius, Aldo climbs the tree he's in and cuts down the branch Cornelius is standing on—causing him to fall.

With his son severely injured and near death, Caesar shuts himself away and stays by Cornelius' bedside until he dies. Aldo takes advantage of Caesar's absence and seizes power; raiding the armory and imprisoning all the humans. And when the army from the Forbidden City is seen approaching Ape City, Aldo and his soldiers mount their horses and ride off to meet them on the battlefield.

The army of the Forbidden City launches a barrage of attacks against Ape City, but Caesar is able to turn the tide of the battle by drawing the soldiers into the city and then fighting them in close-quarter combat. The mutant army is forced to retreat, but is met by Aldo and his soldiers and are killed. When he returns to the city Aldo challenges Caesar for control, but his supporters quickly turn on him when it is revealed that Aldo killed Cornelius by cutting the branch from under him. Surrounded and with nowhere to go, Aldo attempts to escape by climbing up a tree and is chased by Caesar—seeking revenge for his son's death. In a struggle with Caesar, Aldo falls to his death and Caesar realizes that apes aren't superior to man; leading him to free the humans and treat them as equals.

REVIEW

While it's considered one of the weakest of the *Apes* films, *Battle for the Planet of the Apes* is actually quite compelling. With Caesar's segregation of apes and humans, and the humans in the Forbidden City turning into mutants, we see the beginnings of what could grow into the dystopian world of the first film. Or not. With the wraparound story of the Lawgiver, the possibility arises that the *Apes* saga has led to a better future and that the sacrifices throughout have not been in vain.

The writers have done a good job at creating strong characters with some interesting story arcs. And the look and design of the post-war world is rather intriguing; having hints of the ape society of the original film, but also distinctly different. Additionally, the inclusion of the Lawgiver is a real treat for fans; finally meeting (if ever so briefly) this towering figure that looms so large in the apes' culture.

Yet again, the series is able to assemble a number of distinguished actors, including Claude Akins, Paul Williams, and John Huston; who all give strong performances. Huston in particular does a wonderful job—perfectly encapsulating the Lawgiver. And Claude Akins plays a great villain; making Aldo a terrific foil for Caesar. Williams too enriches the material; playing a kinder, more humble version of Dr. Zaius that has a certain charm to him.

Twentieth Century Fox once again undermines the film with their budget cuts; which are felt more in this film than in any of the previous ones. The ape masks for the extras look cheap, and the climactic battle is underwhelming to say the least (which is a problem for a film with "Battle" in the title). And there are some continuity errors (or just story problems in general) in tying the film into the others.

While there are failings to be sure, *Battle for the Planet of the Apes* is a worthy entry into the series. Keeping to the formula, it delivers exciting action sequences along with exploring important social issues. Yet it does so in fresh new ways and doesn't just repeat what has been done before. And the film ties up the series nicely with an ambiguous end scene that can be read as either hopeful or fatalistic.

THE DIVINE SPARK

Battle for the Planet of the Apes is in some ways an Eden parable. Caesar believes that he has created an ideal community, and that ape rule will prevent it from being plagued by the violence and destruction that characterized man's society. But Aldo will soon introduce ape murder; a sin that will shock the apes out of their illusion of being innately morally superior to humans.

And then there is the question of how to deal with a murderer. At the start of the film Caesar wonders if it's "right to kill evil so that good should prevail," and at the end of the film he will have to make that choice when it's revealed that Aldo has killed. It's a dilemma that we still wrestle with. Like the previous films, there is much to explore here.

THOU SHALL NOT KILL

When Aldo arrives at the school house, Abe is teaching a writing lesson using the apes' most fundamental law: Ape shall never kill ape. And Caesar reiterates this as a cornerstone of his people's culture when talking with MacDonald, telling him, "Ape never kills ape." To Caesar, it is what distinguishes ape society from man's society. Having lived through the atomic war that left the world in ruin, Caesar sees killing as a human characteristic that led to man's downfall.

Aldo, however, has a different view of killing than Caesar. Despite the prohibition on killing, Aldo secretly meets with his gorilla soldiers and plots to kill Caesar: "We will smash the humans...and then we will smash Caesar!" Rather than viewing murder as a self-destructive human characteristic, Aldo sees it as a means to gain power. And when his murderous plans are overheard by Caesar's son Cornelius, Aldo attempts to kill him by cutting down the tree branch that Cornelius is holding onto.

God's condemnation of murder is one of the Ten Commandments (number six) and His abhorrence of it appears throughout Scripture. It is so grievous a sin that it calls for the gravest and most severe of punishments.

- Exodus 20:13 – *You shall not murder.*

- Exodus 21:14 – *[I]f anyone schemes and kills someone deliberately, that person is to be taken from my altar and put to death.*

CHAPTER 5

- Leviticus 24:17 – *Anyone who takes the life of a human being is to be put to death.*

- Proverbs 6:16-19 – *There are six things the L<small>ORD</small> hates, seven that are detestable to him: haughty eyes, a lying tongue, hands that shed innocent blood, a heart that devises wicked schemes, feet that are quick to rush into evil, a false witness who pours out lies and a person who stirs up conflict in the community.*

When Caesar attempts to free the humans that Aldo locked inside of a corral, Aldo threatens to kill him. During this confrontation Virgil reveals before all of the assembled apes that Aldo killed Cornelius by cutting the branch that he fell from. The apes then turn on Aldo, realizing that he has violated their "most sacred law," and he attempts to flee by escaping into a tree. But Caesar pursues him and Aldo dies; falling to his death while battling with Caesar.

UNITY

According to the Lawgiver, "God created beast and man so that both might live in friendship and share dominion over a world at peace." But Caesar is not that evolved yet. The community that he has built has a caste system that puts apes above humans; as humans are forbidden to say "no" to an ape, must address apes with respect, and are banned from attending council meetings. Yet, Caesar does have hope that their two peoples, ape and man, can become equals once they have gotten to know and trust each other.

When an army from the Forbidden City attacks, the community divide is exacerbated by Aldo; who rounds up all of the humans and puts them in a corral. Upon seeing this Virgil goes to Caesar, who becomes outraged at seeing what Aldo has done. Following the battle with the Forbidden City's army and the death of Aldo, Caesar orders the humans released. But they are reluctant to go back to being second class citizens, and demand to be equal members of the community going forward; telling Caesar, "If you mean to set us free, than free us completely."

The Scriptures tell us that we are to cast off ethnic and social divides, for we are one in Christ. Our unity in Him overcomes all divisions and makes us kin.

- Romans 10:12 – *For there is no difference between Jew and Gentile—the same Lord is Lord of all and richly blesses all who call on him,*

- 1 Corinthians 12:13 – *For we were all baptized by one Spirit so as to form one body—whether Jews or Gentiles, slave or free—and we were all given the one Spirit to drink.*

- Ephesians 3:6 – *This mystery is that through the gospel the Gentiles are heirs together with Israel, members together of one body, and sharers together in the promise in Christ Jesus.*

- Colossians 3:11 – *Here there is no Gentile or Jew, circumcised or uncircumcised, barbarian, Scythian, slave or free, but Christ is all, and is in all.*

Upon reflection, Caesar realizes his prejudice toward humans and welcomes them back into the community as full and equal members. And 600 years later, we see "apes and humans living in friendship, harmony

CHAPTER 5

and at peace" surrounding the Lawgiver as he tells them the tale of Caesar and how he brought about their unity.

ACCOUNTABILITY

Before Caesar, MacDonald, and Virgil can go on their expedition to the Forbidden City they gather provisions. However, the keeper of the armory, Mandemus, is also "the keeper of Caesar's conscience" and has been empowered by Caesar to grant or deny requests for guns—even from Caesar himself. Thus Mandemus challenges them with a series of questions that must be answered to his satisfaction; proving that their need for arms is legitimate and necessary. Their answers prove to be sufficient, and Mandemus allows them into the armor and gives them the guns that they request.

When Aldo brings a group of his soldiers to raid the armory, he has no time for Mandemus and his questions. When asked what they plan to do with the weapons, Aldo says, "We shall do with them what we will;" which Mandemus calls "the devil's law." Holding themselves accountable to no one, Aldo and his soldiers force their way into the armory and take what they want; ignoring Mandemus' calls to stop and his protestations that what they are doing is unlawful.

In Scripture we are told that we are to be our brother's keeper; to be accountable to and for our fellow brothers and sisters, and that by this we will strengthen and encourage each other onward toward the Lord.

- Proverbs 27:17 – *As iron sharpens iron, so one person sharpens another.*

- Luke 17:3 – *If your brother or sister sins against you, rebuke them; and if they repent, forgive them.*

- Galatians 6:1 – *Brothers and sisters, if someone is caught in a sin, you who live by the Spirit should restore that person gently.*

- Ephesians 5:21 – *Submit to one another out of reverence for Christ.*

When the dust has settled and Caesar is back in power following the battle with the army from the Forbidden City and Aldo's challenge for leadership, all of the weapons are gathered up and returned to the armory and accounted for by Mandemus. And while Mandemus thinks that his services are no longer needed, Caesar tells him to continue in his position. Vigil agrees, telling Mandemus that "[t]he greatest danger of all is that danger never ends."

ALPHA AND OMEGA

Ever since man was driven out of Eden he's tried to get back, or at least tried to return to that state of peace and harmony. But try as we might, in the words of Thomas Wolfe, "You can't go home again." Yet while we may not literally be able to return to Eden, God has laid out a way to get back into union with Him. And that map can be found in the Word.

But before we can return to unity with the Lord, we must be in unity with our brothers and sisters in Christ. We must become one body as a church and overcome the myriad of divisions that the world seeks to impose on us; whether it's race, gender, class, or creed. While God created and loves our uniquenesses, they are not meant to separate and divide us, but rather to bring us together.

Together we grow stronger; sharing our struggles and accomplishments. Holding each other accountable, we are able to keep each other from harm and offer the support that we each need. Accountability also shows our care and concern, and builds a sense of community. And in this way we can start to re-experience some of what was lost in Eden.

We were meant to dwell with the Lord. But to do so we must cast out any anger or violent feelings toward our fellow man, join ourselves to the Church (which is the body of Christ), and take responsibility for our brothers and sisters, recognizing that we are one. Taking these steps will lead us closer to the presence of the Lord and allow us to experience the peace that He offers.

> Colossians 3:15 – *Let the peace of Christ rule in your hearts, since as members of one body you were called to peace. And be thankful.*

"Never send a monkey to do a man's job."

CHAPTER 6: PLANET OF THE APES

Director: Tim Burton
Screenplay: William Broyles Jr. and Lawrence Konner
    & Mark Rosenthal
Cast: Mark Wahlberg as Capt. Leo Davidson
    Tim Roth as Gen. Thade
    Helena Bonham Carter as Ari
    Michael Clarke Duncan as Col. Attar
    Kris Kristofferson as Karubi
    Estella Warren as Daena
    Paul Giamatti as Limbo

PLOT

In the near future the *Oberon* space station is conducting research using genetically modified apes to pilot space-pods. When the station comes across an electromagnetic storm a chimp named Pericles is sent to investigate, but his pod is lost in the storm. Capt. Leo Davison refuses to abandon the chimp and follows him into the storm in another pod, but ends up crash-landing on a strange planet.

    Davidson finds himself in an unknown jungle among primitive humans. Then, to his horror, traps start springing and hunters descend upon him and the other humans. He tries to evade the hunters, but is soon captured and discovers that they are large, talking apes dressed in uniforms and carrying weapons.

CHAPTER 6

Rounded up with the other humans, Davidson is taken to the apes' city and is sold into bondage by a slave trader.

When an opportunity presents itself, Davidson breaks free of his cage and releases the other humans he's imprisoned with, and leads them out of the city under the cover of night. During the escape he's caught by his ape master Ari and her servant. But Davidson is able to convince her to let him go and promises to show her his spacecraft. Upon reaching his pod he's able to retrieve several pieces of equipment and discovers that the *Oberon* is nearby and sending out a homing signal.

To get to the *Oberon*, Davidson and his group head to a forbidden area that the apes call Calima and sneak pass an ape garrison that blocks their path. Upon learning of the escape, Gen. Thade mounts an army and marches to Calima. Ari attempts to broker a peace, but is rebuffed by Thade; who brands her as a human and promises death and destruction for all who side with Davidson and his rebellion.

When Davidson reaches the *Oberon*, he finds it in ruins and learns that they were sucked into the same electromagnetic storm that he was and emerged thousands of years earlier and crashed; and that the genetically engineered apes killed them. With his hope of rescue gone, Davidson joins the bands of humans that have come to Calima to stand against the apes. A battle between the ape army and the humans ensues, but abruptly ends when Pericles lands his pod in the middle of the battlefield. And when Davidson explains the true origins of how the apes and humans came to the planet, Thade's second in command abandons him and declares peace with the humans. Davidson then detects a reappearance of the space storm and launches in Pericles' pod, and returns home to Earth; but after crash-landing in Washington D.C., he discovers that it's not the Earth that he left, and that it is now ruled by apes.

REVIEW

One of the first "re-imaginings" (as opposed to a remake) of a classic film, Tim Burton's *Planet of the Apes* returns to the original Pierre Boulle novel and looks for a different story than the one Serling and Wilson came up with. And those familiar with the novel will recognize that the '68 version was not especially faithful to the source material; leaving room for other cinematic interpretations. That said, Burton goes a little too out of his way to avoid redoing what the '68 version did (to the film's detriment).

The casting is pretty impressive: Mark Wahlberg, Tim Roth, Helena Bonham Carter, Paul Giamatti. However, the actors in the ape makeup seem to give the better performances—Roth especially. The ape makeup is again an amazing feat and a highlight of the film; anthropomorphizing apes as never before. And in a nice nod to the original, Charlton Heston and Linda Harrison are each given cameos; Heston even gets to reprise his famous "damn them" line from the original.

But sadly the storytelling is quite poor, doing a particularly bad job at developing the characters—especially Davidson. Davidson is woefully underdeveloped and makes for a rather unsympathetic hero that seems more interested in getting off the planet than in helping his fellow humans. And all the science comes off as gobbledygook; which makes it difficult to go along with the gene manipulation, electromagnetic storm, and time-travel.

On the other hand, Burdon delivers more intense and exciting action scenes than any of the original series films ever attempted (save for *Conquest*). And unlike in the original series, the apes fight like apes—making full use of their strength and dexterity. Yet any goodwill that the film engenders is undone by the inexplicable "twist" ending that comes out of nowhere and has nothing to do with the plot.

Remaking a classic of the caliber of the '68 *Planet of the Apes* really is an impossibly task. However, Burton is able to deliver a bold and exciting vision that (if nothing else) reignited interest in the franchise and the ideas that it presented. Flawed as it is, the 2001 *Planet of the Apes* explores the same issues of inequality, social injustice, and civil rights that the original did. For all its differences and failings, it got the core of what the series is about right.

THE DIVINE SPARK

Tim Burton's *Planet of the Apes* has a strong leadership theme throughout the character arcs. Capt. Leo Davidson begins as a bit of a rogue, disobeying orders and doing things his own way, but circumstances will lead him to take up the mantle of leadership when a revolution forms around him. Gen. Thade also deals with issues of leadership. An insecure leader, Thade uses manipulation to get what he wants and to solidify his power; and his power and position are threatened when Davison arrivals and goes looking for answers at

Calima that could unravel the lies that Thade's family's claim to power is based on.

The examples that these two set will affect others. Ari leaves the safety of being a senator's daughter and becomes a renegade; joining Davison and attempting to sacrifice herself for his safety. And Col. Attar will see Thade for who he really is, sacrificing soldiers for his own glory and covering up the lies of his family, and choices to abandon Thade and lead the apes and humans into a new future as equals. But there are also many other themes and issues explored in this rich and provocative film.

GOOD SHEPHERD

As the *Oberon* space station investigates an electromagnetic storm, Capt. Leo Davidson works with his ape pilot Pericles—running him through a simulator. When Pericles fails, Davidson ends the simulation and tries to instruct Pericles on what he did wrong and what he should have done differently. But he doesn't just criticize Pericles for what he did wrong; Davidson also rewards him for his effort by giving him a sugar cube.

After some initial scans, the commander of the *Oberon* decides to send out an ape piloted pod to investigate the storm. Davidson escorts Pericles to a pod and guides him through his flight sequence. But shortly after entering the disturbance, the pod goes off course and the commander considers Pericles lost. However, Davidson refuses to give up on Pericles and disobeys his commanding officer; telling him that he's "goin' to get [his] chimp."

In Scripture the imagery of a shepherd is often used to describe how the Lord looks after us. It is also used

CHAPTER 6

as an example of how we are to look after those He has placed in our care.

- Proverbs 27:23 – *Be sure you know the condition of your flocks, give careful attention to your herds*

- Jeremiah 3:15 – *Then I will give you shepherds after my own heart, who will lead you with knowledge and understanding.*

- John 10:14 – *I am the good shepherd; I know my sheep and my sheep know me*

- Acts 20:28 – *Keep watch over yourselves and all the flock of which the Holy Spirit has made you overseers. Be shepherds of the church of God, which he bought with his own blood.*

When Pericles makes his landing at Calima and is mistaken for Semos, his life is in danger. Thade recognizes the threat Pericles represents (exposing the truth of the apes' origins) and chases him into the *Oberon* wreckage. Davidson attempts to stop Thade, but Pericles is wounded in the ensuing fight. With his home destroyed and his fellow apes from the *Oberon* gone, Pericles has nowhere to go. But Davidson finds a new home for him with Ari; who comforts Pericles and promises to care for him.

PRAYER

Senator Sandar holds a formal dinner and invites Gen. Thade, Col. Attar, and other honored guests. Once the table is set one of the guests starts to eat, but Attar objects to this and insists that they pray first. He then leads the table in a prayer to Semos, their religious deity: "We give thanks to you, Semos, for the fruit of the land. Bless us, holy Father, who created all apes in his image. Hasten the day when you will return and bring peace to your children. Amen."

Later, when the human slaves escape from the city, Col. Attar assumes command of an army outpost; believing that the humans will be coming that way. Later in the evening Attar retires to his tent, and within the tent Attar has set up an altar with a religious painting and a statue of Semos, and again he offers prayers—seeking strength and guidance in the task he's been given. But his prayers are interrupted when the humans attempt a daring night raid through the ape's encampment to cross a river.

We are told throughout Scripture to pray to the Lord; that it is a vital part of our relationship with Him. Through it we grow closer to Him and each other, and learn to hear His voice.

- Ephesians 6:18 – *And pray in the Spirit on all occasions with all kinds of prayers and requests. With this in mind, be alert and always keep on praying for all the Lord's people.*

- Philippians 4:6-7 – *Do not be anxious about anything, but in every situation, by prayer and petition, with thanksgiving, present your requests to God. And the peace of God, which transcends all understanding, will guard your hearts and your minds in Christ Jesus.*

- Colossians 4:2 – *Devote yourselves to prayer, being watchful and thankful.*

CHAPTER 6

- 1 Timothy 2:8 – *Therefore I want the men everywhere to pray, lifting up holy hands without anger or disputing.*

In the middle of the battle at Calima between the apes and the humans an object suddenly appears in the sky accompanied by a loud boom. It is a space-pod from the *Oberon*, and fighting ceases as everyone waits to see who or what will come out. When the pod door opens it reveals an ape, and at seeing this Attar leads the apes in blowing down in supplication and offers prayers of gratitude for the return of who he believes to be Semos; declaring, "The prophecy is true. Semos has returned to us."

LEADERSHIP

Upon breaking out of his cage, Capt. Leo Davidson takes charge of the escape from Ape City. And when he's caught by Ari, he's able to convince her to let them go by making a deal to show her "something that will change [her] world forever"—his space-pod. He also manages a fragile truce between the humans who have just broken free of their bondage and the apes that have come along. Davidson's fierce determination and confidence holds the company together.

Word of Davidson's defiance of the apes and harrowing journey to Calima spreads, and soon leads hundreds of humans to rally to Davidson. At first Davidson is overwhelmed by this unexpected turn of events, but soon comes to recognize the need that they have for a leader. And reluctantly he accepts the responsibility placed on him, and begins to plan for the inevitable battle that will come when Gen. Thade and his army catches up to him.

The Scriptures are full of guidance for how to be a good leader. Among other things, those who wish to lead should be selfless, honest, and dedicated to serving others.

- Exodus 18:21 – *[S]elect capable men from all the people—men who fear God, trustworthy men who hate dishonest gain—and appoint them as officials over thousands, hundreds, fifties and tens.*

- 1 Timothy 3:2 – *Now the overseer is to be above reproach, faithful to his wife, temperate, self-controlled, respectable, hospitable, able to teach,*

- Titus 1:7 – *Since an overseer manages God's household, he must be blameless—not overbearing, not quick-tempered, not given to drunkenness, not violent, not pursuing dishonest gain.*

- 1 Peter 5:2 – *Be shepherds of God's flock that is under your care, watching over them—not because you must, but because you are willing, as God wants you to be; not pursuing dishonest gain, but eager to serve;*

At Calima Davidson learns that the humans on the planet are descendants of the *Oberon* crew, who crashed there after passing through the same electromagnetic storm that brought him there. As the ape army nears, he offers encouragement to the gathered humans; telling them, "Our history is filled with men

CHAPTER 6

who have done amazing things. That history belongs to you now." And that "[s]ometimes even a few can make a difference." Looking to protect them and keep as many of them out of harm's way as possible, Davidson devises a plan to demonstrate the power of the *Oberon*—hoping that it will convince Thade to stop his attack.

ALPHA AND OMEGA

Until the Lord returns, we, His people, will need leaders to help to support and guide us. And He has laid in the hearts of the chosen to take on this responsibility. Some feel the call and answer without reservation, while others are reluctant and must be cajoled into accepting. But not all who seek the responsibility of leadership do it for the right reasons or are fit to serve.

A true leader of God is a Good Shepherd who looks after the needs of those in his or her charge. As American statesman Sam Houston once said, "A leader is someone who helps improve the lives of others." Staying on the straight and narrow path is hard, and it's easy to get lost and confused. And a good leader will be there to help us get through the difficult times and to set us back on course should we stray. Additionally, the Body of Christ is made up of many different kinds of people with different needs, and an effective leader must serve those needs so that each community can fulfill the mission God has laid out for them.

Prayer is also a part of being a Godly leader. Those who take on the responsibility of leading God's people must continually seek His will and be an intercessor for the needs and wellbeing of those in their care. But leaders also need the prayers of their congregants, for they too need the strength and rejuvenation that comes through prayer. And the more we open up to God, the more He becomes a part of our lives.

No leader is perfect, and we must be vigilant; lest a bad leader lead the flock astray. Yet we shouldn't fear placing ourselves under the stewardship of righteous men and women that God has called to shepherd His people. Nor should we fear the call to leadership if the Lord places it in our hearts. For the Lord is the Good Shepherd, and is tending to our needs and will not leave us aimless in His absence.

> Hebrews 13:7 – *Remember your leaders, who spoke the word of God to you. Consider the outcome of their way of life and imitate their faith.*

"Caesar is home."

CHAPTER 7: RISE OF THE PLANET OF THE APES

Director: Rupert Wyatt
Screenplay: Rick Jaffa & Amanda Silver
Cast: Andy Serkis as Caesar
James Franco as Will Rodman
Freida Pinto as Caroline Aranha
John Lithgow as Charles Rodman
Brian Cox as John Landon
Tom Felton as Dodge Landon
David Oyelowo as Steven Jacobs

PLOT

Gen-Sys genetic researcher Dr. Will Rodman is working to cure Alzheimer's disease and other cognitive disorders. But when one of the research subjects, a chimpanzee named Bright Eyes, breaks loose and attacks several employees the project is shut down. However, when it's discovered that Bright Eyes had had a baby and was protecting her young, Rodman decides to take the orphaned chimp home and raises it.

Before long Rodman discovers that the young chimp, which his father names Caesar, is showing advanced intelligence and cognitive abilities beyond what normal apes are capable of. He determines that Caesar's increased abilities are due to the experimental drug ALZ-112 that his mother was given, and decides to use the drug on his father—who is suffering from Alzheimer's. Overnight the disease goes into remission and Rodman's father regains his mental acuity.

Rodman then takes the data that he's collected from his father's recovery to his supervisor at Gen-Sys and he agrees to restart the ALZ-112 program. Meanwhile, Caesar starts to become aware that he's different; and when he gets into an altercation with a neighbor while defending Rodman's father (who's starting to relapse), Caesar is send away to a primate sanctuary.

At first Caesar is unhappy living with the other apes and only thinks about going back home with Rodman. But eventual he comes to see them as his people and chooses to stay when Rodman comes to take him home. However, Caesar recognizes that the other apes aren't as intelligent as him and lack unity. So he sneaks out to Rodman's house to steal canisters of the new ALZ-113 drug Rodman's been working on and exposes the sanctuary apes to it. He also takes over as alpha and shows the apes how to work together.

When one of the sanctuary workers attempts to beat Caesar with an electric prod after finding him outside of his cage, Caesar stands up to him and says, "No!" Caesar then leads an escape from the sanctuary and goes to free the apes at Gen-Sys that are being experimented on. Then together they all go to the city zoo to break out the apes being held there. Once he has freed all the apes, Caesar heads toward the Redwood Forrest. But the police set up a blockade on the Golden Gate Bridge and a fight ensues. The apes are victorious and disappear into the forest, but not before Rodman catches up and bits goodbye to Caesar.

CHAPTER 7
REVIEW

A true spiritual successor to the original, *Rise of the Planet of the Apes* pushes the technological boundaries of filmmaking, addresses controversial social issues, and tells a compelling story. The decision to start with an origin story (a popular trend at the time it was made) is exactly what the franchise needed. And, it both honors the original film series while building something new and exciting.

As with the previous films, it all starts with getting the right actors; and this is all the more important when dealing with motion capture. In fact, many of the ape performers will return for the whole trilogy. Andy Serkis (of *Lord of the Rings* fame) is incredibly skilled and brings Caesar to life; incorporating expressions and gestures that raises the character above a normal CGI creation. And the cast that play the human characters are quite talented as well: James Franco, John Lithgow, Brian Cox.

The controversial choice to use CGI motion capture for the apes instead of makeup (as the past films did) was incredibly bold and the film is better for it. While there are a few seams showing, for the most part the CGI apes are extraordinarily realistic and allow for some remarkable scenes; particularly in the fight sequences. And the action itself is dynamic and thrilling.

However, the film doesn't shy away from the social commentary that is a hallmark of *Apes* films. But rather than recycle the same issues that the original series dealt with, it tackles some of the more pertinent topics of the 21st century—medical ethics, animal rights, genetic manipulation. Yet the film never lets them overshadow the story of Caesar discovering who he is and finding his place in the world; a theme that speaks to all of us in some way.

Rise of the Planet of the Apes re-envisions the Caesar story from *Conquest of the Planet of the Apes* in a way that pays tribute to the franchise's past but also reshapes the franchise for a new generation. And it does so without compromising what the series is about. A thrilling and smart sci-fi adventure, *Rise of the Planet of the Apes* provides a solid foundation on which to relaunch the franchise.

THE DIVINE SPARK

Rise of the Planet of the Apes starts a new chapter in the series, and with it comes new issues and themes to explore. Unlike the original series mythology, here the origin of the intelligent ape comes from an altruistic place—a desire to do good through healing. Dr. Will Rodman is a healer, and his efforts to cure diseases will give birth to intelligent apes. Similarly, Caesar attempts to do good by being a uniter, and his efforts to unite the apes will give birth to a revolution.

Our actions often have unintended consequences; sometimes they're positive, sometimes they're negative. Both Will and Caesar will have to face those consequences. The road to hell is said to be paved with good intentions, and Will and Caesar both started on their roads with good intentions. But will their roads lead to perdition or salvation, or both? The film opens up a host of moral and ethical issues to explore, and explore them it does.

CHAPTER 7
HEALING

Dr. Will Rodman is working with apes at Gen-Sys in an attempt to find a cure to mental disorders. Having a father with Alzheimer's, he has been personally affected by such disorders. When Rodman makes his presentation on the drug that he's been developing, ALZ-112, he focuses on its regenerative, healing properties; telling the board that the drug "can be used to treat a wide range of brain disorders" and that its potential is "virtually limitless."

A compassionate man, Rodman takes pity on Bright Eyes' newborn ape when he's discovered and takes him home to raise instead of euthanizing. And when he sees the effects that ALZ-112 has had on the ape, who is given the name Caesar, Rodman begins treating his father with the drug. Rodman's father soon starts to recover from his Alzheimer's and regains his mental faculties. He's able to play the piano again and helps to care for Caesar.

Our God is a God of healing. The Scriptures record numerous healings throughout Christ's ministry, and we are called to carry on that ministry; to heal in His name for the glory of God.

- Matthew 10:1 – *Jesus called his twelve disciples to him and gave them authority to drive out impure spirits and to heal every disease and sickness.*

- Luke 13:13 – *Then [Jesus] put his hands on her, and immediately she straightened up and praised God.*

- Acts 4:30 – *Stretch out your hand to heal and perform signs and wonders through the name of your holy servant Jesus.*

- James 5:14-15 – *Is anyone among you sick? Let them call the elders of the church to pray over them and anoint them with oil in the name of the Lord. And the prayer offered in faith will make the sick person well; the Lord will raise them up. If they have sinned, they will be forgiven.*

However, Dr. Rodman soon discovers that the effects of the ALZ-112 drug aren't permanent; as his father's health begins to decline and the Alzheimer's returns. But he takes the data that he's collected from his father's temporary recovery and makes another pitch to his boss at Gen-Sys to restart the ALZ-112 program; hoping to make a stronger drug that will help his father. The pitch is successful and new testing of a revised drug, ALZ-113, begins.

MONEY IS THE ROOT OF EVIL

Steven Jacobs, the director of Gen-Sys, prioritizes profits over ethics. Immediately after Bright Eyes attacks the Gen-Sys board Jacobs shuts down the ALZ-112 program, deeming it a failure, and is unwilling to expend any more resources on it—even to determine if the cause of Bright Eyes' aggressive episode was related to the drug or not. Seeing nothing to gain, he has all of the apes euthanized; telling the ape handler to "[f]ind the most cost-effective way to put [the] apes down."

Things change however when Dr. Rodman pitches the ALZ program again a few years later; this time with

CHAPTER 7

the preliminary research already conducted privately by Rodman. When he's told that the drug shows signs of "[improving] cognitive functioning [and] memory quality" Jacobs immediately sees the profit potential in the various uses of a revised ALZ-112. He even fast-tracks the drug's testing and bypasses the normal development procedures when he sees the results on a test subject named Koba (and this will have deadly consequences).

Scripture warns us repeatedly about the dangers of money. Not that it is evil in and of itself, but that it has tremendous power to corrupt and to lure us away from the Lord and His service.

- Ecclesiastes 5:10 – *Whoever loves money never has enough; whoever loves wealth is never satisfied with their income.*

- Matthew 6:24 – *No one can serve two masters. Either you will hate the one and love the other, or you will be devoted to the one and despise the other. You cannot serve both God and money.*

- 1 Timothy 6:9-10 – *Those who want to get rich fall into temptation and a trap and into many foolish and harmful desires that plunge people into ruin and destruction. For the love of money is a root of all kinds of evil. Some people, eager for money, have wandered from the faith and pierced themselves with many griefs.*

- Hebrews 13:5 – *Keep your lives free from the love of money and be content with what you have, because God has said, "Never will I leave you; never will I forsake you."*

In the rush to test the new drug ALZ-113 an accident occurs in the labs in which an employee is exposed to a massive dose of the drug and is not quarantined. Infected with ALZ-113, the employee spreads the virus to others he comes in contact with—unleashing a deadly outbreak. Furthermore, Jacobs ignores warnings from Rodman about the rushed testing; countering his arguments with the profit making potential of the drug. And as a result of the lax standards of Jacobs, Koba, the subject of multiple experimentations that have left him permanently scarred, is put into the ALZ-113 program and he unleash his hatred of humans when he's freed during Caesar's attack on Gen-Sys—ultimately resulting in Jacobs death.

STRONGER TOGETHER

When Caesar first gets to the primate sanctuary, he has trouble socializing and fitting in with the other apes—finding only one friend in a circus orangutan named Maurice. The alpha chimpanzee Rocket quickly establishes dominance, and Caesar is content to stay on the periphery and wait for Rodman to come for him and take him home. But over time he begins to see himself as part of this community of apes and grows distressed over the mistreatment that is taking place.

Caesar uses Buck, a gorilla, to get Rocket to submit to his authority and becomes the new alpha. He then teaches Rocket to share with the other apes—building a sense of equality and unity. As Caesar tells his friend Maurice during one of their talks, "Apes alone weak.

CHAPTER 7

Apes together strong." Eventually, working together, the apes are able to break out of the sanctuary. And they stay together as a group with the common goal of making it out of the city and to freedom.

We too are to work as a community. Throughout Scripture the Lord tells us to live, work, and worship as a community and warns against separating and dividing ourselves.

- Genesis 2:18 – *The Lord God said, "It is not good for the man to be alone."*

- Ecclesiastes 4:9-10 – *Two are better than one, because they have a good return for their labor: If either of them falls down, one can help the other up. But pity anyone who falls and has no one to help them up.*

- Galatians 6:2 – *Carry each other's burdens, and in this way you will fulfill the law of Christ.*

- Hebrews 10:24-25 – *And let us consider how we may spur one another on toward love and good deeds, not giving up meeting together, as some are in the habit of doing, but encouraging one another—and all the more as you see the Day approaching.*

Unwilling to leave any of his fellow apes in captivity, Caesar leads his group to Gen-Sys; which had been taking apes from the sanctuary for experimentation. From there the apes go the city zoo and free more of their brothers and sisters. Sensing the power and purpose of this rogue band of apes, the zoo apes join them. Having grown his small sanctuary group into an army,

Caesar leads the apes to their final obstacle, the Golden Gate Bridge; where squads of police await prepared to put down Caesar's rebellion. But working together, the apes are able to overcome the police and make it to the Redwood Forrest where they disappear into the trees.

ALPHA AND OMEGA

Edward A. Murphy is credited with coining the phrase, "Anything that can go wrong will go wrong"—Murphy's Law. It's something that nearly everyone has experienced at some time or another. And our efforts to do good and minister for Christ are not immune to it. As pure as our intentions, and as led by the Spirit as we may feel, things will not always turn out as we imagined or hoped. But the good news is, as wrong as our efforts may turn out sometimes, the Lord can use them and work things for the good.

One thing that often corrupts our efforts is money. The love of money has led many souls astray; particularly in the Church. Success and growth will often go wrong, leading people away from Christ; compromising biblical values in order to reach more people and do more ministry. More money also whettens the taste for expensive things and excesses; taking a person away from humbleness and reliance on God. While money can be a blessed thing, it's also likely to create its own set of problems.

Taking too much upon oneself is also a common way in which we turn our plans to folly. We are always stronger together and the Lord has called us to be a community that bares each other's burdens. Working as one, in unity, the Church can, and has, accomplished

CHAPTER 7

great things. And it is only by putting Christ first, above our own pride, that we can accomplish those things and truly bring Him glory.

Whether or not we succeed or fail ultimately comes down to trust—our trust in each other and in God. Succeeding without God isn't really success, and failing with God isn't really failing. He tells us in the Word not to rely on our own understanding (Proverbs 3:5). Just because a thing doesn't turn out the way we foresaw it doesn't mean that it's gone wrong. If we are putting the Lord first and seeking His glory, than He will bless our works.

> Matthew 6:21 – *For where your treasure is, there your heart will be also.*

"Ape always seek strongest branch."

CHAPTER 8: DAWN OF THE PLANET OF THE APES

Director: Matt Reeves
Screenplay: Mark Bomback and
  Rick Jaffa & Amanda Silver
Cast: Andy Serkis as Caesar
  Jason Clarke as Malcolm
  Gary Oldman as Dreyfus
  Keri Russell as Ellie
  Toby Kebbell as Koba
  Nick Thurston as Blue Eyes

Plot

In the years since Caesar lead his revolt, a plague known as the Simian Flu has wiped out most of mankind and society has fallen. However, a group of survivors have banded together and build a community shelter in the ruins of San Francisco. Running low on resources, they send a scouting party into the Redwood Forest to find an old hydroelectric power station to see if it can be repaired.

While trekking through the forest, they run into a group of intelligent, speaking apes. After a brief skirmish Caesar tells the humans to leave. The next day he marches an ape army to the San Francisco shelter in a show of force and publicly announces that the forest is ape territory and that they won't allow any further encroachments. Despite this, Malcolm, one of the leaders

CHAPTER 8

of the San Francisco community, puts together a team to go to Caesar and negotiate a deal to allow them to fix the power station.

Caesar and Malcolm eventually come to terms, and the humans are given three days to work on the power station under ape supervision. This decision enrages one of Caesar's senior lieutenants, Koba, who is deeply distrustful of humans and resents them for experimenting on him in animal testing labs. Believing that Caesar is blind to the dangers of humans, Koba attempts to assassinate Caesar and places blame on the human workers; who flee for their lives when they realize what has happened.

Koba then rallies the apes to attack the human shelter in San Francisco. They quickly take the shelter and kill or imprison the remaining humans. Koba then turns on Caesar's supporters and begins imprisoning them; and any other ape who disobeys his orders. Erstwhile, Malcolm finds a wounded Caesar in the forest and nurses him back to health.

Malcolm and Caesar then work together to put Caesar back into power so that he can stop Koba. Caesar's son Blue Eyes joins them and rallies Caesar's supporters and coordinates a breakout. Once freed, they join Caesar and head to the central tower of the city where all the apes have congregated. Meanwhile, Malcolm stumbles upon a human resistance cell that's planning to take out the apes by blowing-up the tower, and he tries to stop them. In an ensuing standoff, one of the resistance fighters succeeds in igniting several explosives that partially collapses the tower. But the standoff with Malcolm buys Caesar time to challenge Koba for leadership, and in their fight Koba is killed. Yet despite this victory, the human resistance was able to send out a call for help and the military is on its way. Recognizing that war has begun, Malcolm and Caesar part ways and walk off into an uncertain future.

REVIEW

Dawn of the Planet of the Apes equals or surpasses its predecessor, taking this new vision for the series into fresh and exciting territory. It's the first time that the apes and the humans have been on equal terms; without one being the dominate species. They're both survivors of a collapsed society, building anew. And inevitably they clash—as burgeoning cultures often do.

As per usual, the film assembles a fine cast. Aside from the returning ape performers (Andy Serkis, Karin Konoval, etc.), Jason Clarke, Gary Oldman, and Keri Russell join the cast as the humans; however, their performances are mostly serviceable. Though to be fair, the plot is focused more on the ape community and doesn't give the human characters much to do. The ape actors on the other hand, take their performances up a notch from the last film, seeming more expressive—allowing for greater characterization.

The special effects work has improved as well. The CGI apes are not only photorealistic, but lifelike; moving and interacting with the foreground almost seamlessly. And this serves to heighten the action sequences; bringing a visceral quality to the fight scenes and making them more dynamic. Additionally, the production designs are quite creative; crafting an entirely new vision of Ape City as well as a post-apocalyptic San Francisco.

Yet in all of this, the social commentary hallmark of the series hasn't been forgotten or neglected; Caesar realizes his own prejudices and how they led to his downfall, and that his people have not healed from their mistreatment at the hands of humans. The ethics of war are explored, as is gun culture. The writing (at least in this aspect) is rather ambitious and does a good job at incorporating social issues without coming off as didactic or heavy-handed.

In many ways, *Dawn of the Planet of the Apes* improves on what was begun in *Rise* and takes it to the next level. It answers the challenge laid down by its predecessors and continues the tradition of offering through-provoking science-fiction and thrilling adventures. One of the best entries in the franchise, *Dawn of the Planet of the Apes* is filmmaking at its best.

THE DIVINE SPARK

Once again Planet of the Apes barrows from itself as *Dawn of the Planet of the Apes* looks to revisit some of the themes from the original series film *Battle for the Planet of the Apes*: this time with more of a focus on betrayal. What is betrayal? And can betrayal be the right thing to do? Koba will turn on Caesar when it looks to him as if Caesar has betrayed the apes by putting the humans' needs before the safety of the ape community. Likewise, Malcolm will turn on his fellow humans to give Caesar a chance to regain leadership of the apes and deescalate the march toward an intractable war.

Did Caesar betray his people? Did Malcolm betray his? Or were they simply living out their principles in a difficult situation. This is of particular relevance to the new Christian who must turn his back on a previous life of worldliness. Christ warned us in Matthew 10:35 that we may have to remove ourselves from the life and people we love in order to follow Him. These and other ethical questions are explored in this entry of the new *Apes* saga.

BLESSED ARE THE PEACEMAKERS

After 10 years without seeing any humans, the apes discover a human scouting party in their forest that is looking to fix a hydroelectric power station. Caesar allows them to leave unharmed but then marches with his army to the human shelter in San Francisco and tells them never to return. However, the San Francisco survivors are in a desperate situation and are running low on resources. Wanting to avoid an armed conflict with the apes over the power station in their territory, Malcolm risks his life, defying Caesar's warnings to stay away, in order to broker a peaceful solution.

Eventually Caesar agrees to hear Malcolm's proposal and comes to see that the humans are desperate and that a violent conflict could erupt if a solution cannot be found. Wanting to avoid any more violence with the humans, Caesar tells the apes, "We have one chance for peace. Let them do their human work," and agrees to allow a small group of humans to work on the power station under ape supervision, conditioned on them surrender their weapons.

CHAPTER 8

Throughout Scripture we are called to be peacemakers. While conflict is not always avoidable, the Lord has commanded that we make every effort at peace, and that peace should be our goal.

- Proverbs 12:20 – *Deceit is in the hearts of those who plot evil, but those who promote peace have joy.*

- Psalm 34:14 – *Turn from evil and do good; seek peace and pursue it.*

- Matthew 5:9 – *Blessed are the peacemakers, for they will be called children of God.*

- Hebrews 12:14 – *Make every effort to live in peace with everyone and to be holy; without holiness no one will see the Lord.*

When a human technician named Carver is discovered trying to sneak in a gun, the fragile truce is shaken. But Malcolm's unwilling to give up on this hope for peace, and is able to convince Caesar to give them a second change. Work on the power station is allowed to continue, and to move the work along and speed the humans on their way, Caesar has his apes help. As the apes and humans work together alongside each other, they begin to develop a respect and understanding of one another.

HATRED

Since his mistreatment at the hands of humans as a test subject that left him permanently scared, Koba has hated humans. And when a group of humans are found in the apes' forest, he counsels Caesar to take action against them; telling him that they "[m]ust attack them now! Before they attack us!" Koba's hatred soon leads to a schism between him and Caesar; resulting in bitter arguments. Blinded by his hatred, Koba is unable to put the safety of the ape community ahead of his own dislike and mistrust of humans.

Likewise, Carver is unable to put aside his hatred of apes. Blaming them for the Simian Flu that claimed the lives of his loved ones, he refuses to entrust his safety to them. In violation of the truce Malcolm secured with Caesar, Carver brings a gun with him to the power station. And in doing so, nearly derails the project—jeopardizing the lives of every survivor in the San Francisco shelter.

Hate is a powerful emotion. And we learn from Scripture that hate often leads to destructive ends—causing pain and grief. Thus the Lord warns us to free ourselves of hatred and its ill effects on our lives.

- Proverbs 10:12 – *Hatred stirs up conflict, but love covers over all wrongs.*

- Proverbs 10:18 – *Whoever conceals hatred with lying lips and spreads slander is a fool.*

- Ephesians 4:31 – *Get rid of all bitterness, rage and anger, brawling and slander, along with every form of malice.*

- 1 John 2:11 – *[A]nyone who hates a brother or sister is in the darkness and walks around in the darkness. They do not know where they are going, because the darkness has blinded them.*

In the end, Koba's hatred costs him everything. He burns down the apes' village to goad them into attacking the humans in San Francisco and taking their

CHAPTER 8

shelter. In the process many apes are killed, and Koba begins imprisoning or killing any apes who refuse to follow him; which leads to a rebellion that will take his life. Similarly, Carver's hatred for the apes leads to his separation from the human encampment, and leaves him vulnerable to an attack by Koba that kills him.

BETRAYAL

In the years since their liberation, Caesar and Koba have become close. A top lieutenant, Koba helps lead the apes' hunts and is a trusted advisor. But Koba adamantly opposes Caesar's decision to allow human's into their territory, and openly challenges Caesar's priorities and loyalty to the ape community; accusing him of "put[ting] apes in danger" and "lov[ing] humans more than apes." And while he feigns an apology to Caesar when he's publicly challenged, Koba continues to undermine him; going off to the human city in secret and killing two armory guards.

After stealing a gun, Koba plots to kill Caesar. During a celebration of the completion of the hydroelectric power station repairs, Kuba shoots Caesar and plants evidence that will lead to the humans. He also uses Caesar's son Blue Eyes—making sure that he finds the planted evidence to make the setup all the more convincing. Koba further covers up his attempted assassination of Caesar by setting the apes' home on fire; so that it will look like part of a coordinated attack by the humans.

The Lord wants His people to be honest and upright with Him, and with each other. To that end Scripture is full of condemnations for, and warnings of, betrayal—

the most notorious being that of Christ being betrayed by one of His own disciples.

- 1 Chronicles 12:17 – *David went out to meet them and said to them, "If you have come to me in peace to help me, I am ready for you to join me. But if you have come to betray me to my enemies when my hands are free from violence, may the God of our ancestors see it and judge you."*

- Proverbs 25:9-10 – *If you take your neighbor to court, do not betray another's confidence, or the one who hears it may shame you and the charge against you will stand.*

- Isaiah 16:3 – *Make your shadow like night—at high noon. Hide the fugitives, do not betray the refugees.*

- Luke 22:22 – *The Son of Man will go as it has been decreed. But woe to that man who betrays him!*

Koba's betrayal of Caesar is just the beginning. He soon starts to turn on all his former friends. When Ash refuses Koba's orders to kill, Koba drags him up a flight of stairs and throws him over the railing to his death. He then begins imprisoning anyone he suspects of being loyal to Caesar and his teachings. This soon leads to a fracturing of the community, as Blue Eyes rallies Caesar's allies and organizes a counterstrike to take back leadership of the apes; culminating in a one-on-one fight between Koba and Caesar.

CHAPTER 8
ALPHA AND OMEGA

Ever since the Garden of Eden man has had to deal with betrayal: betraying others, betraying God, betraying ourselves. And without fail it has led to sorrow and destruction: it led to man's expulsion from Eden, the fall of Israel, and the crucifixion of the Son of God. As Ayn Rand once wrote, "Man has the power to act as his own destroyer—and that is the way he has acted through most of his history." To live as God wants us, we must cast out all deceit and live upright lives—be the example to the world of the true path.

To do this we must overcome hate. Hate is a powerful weapon that the devil can use against us to divide us and turn us against each other. God's perfect love cannot penetrate a heart that holds in hate. It taints everything, which is why we are commanded to "[f]irst go and be reconciled" with our brothers and sisters before offering gifts to the Lord (Matthew 5:23-24). God will not be mocked, and if we claim to be sharing His love with the world while clinging to our hate, that's exactly what we will be doing.

We are to be peacemakers. It takes strength and sacrifice, but we can rise above our differences and find compromises that lead to benefits for all. Putting others before ourselves is fundamental to Christ's teachings; as is forgiveness and reconciliation. Of course there are those who will reject our efforts and force confrontations, but we are still beholden to make every effort to find a peaceful solution.

The Lord has called us to be His emissaries to a broken world in need of His love. But we cannot do this if we break trust and betray our principles and each other. If we do not operate in good faith we will never be the shining city on the hill that we are called to be. As difficult as it may seem sometimes, the path of honesty and truthfulness is the one that we must take. For in the end, it is the only way to build faith and trust with each other, our communities, and God.

> Proverbs 11:3 – *The integrity of the upright guides them, but the unfaithful are destroyed by their duplicity.*

"All of human history has led to this moment."

CHAPTER 9: WAR FOR THE PLANET OF THE APES

Director: Matt Reeves
Screenplay: Mark Bomback & Matt Reeves
Cast: Andy Serkis as Caesar
　　　Woody Harrelson as The Colonel
　　　Steve Zahn as Bad Ape
　　　Karin Konoval as Maurice
　　　Terry Notary as Rocket
　　　Amiah Miller as Nova

Plot

On the run from the military, Caesar has sent out scouts to look for a place for the apes to set up a new home after having left San Francisco. The scouts return and inform Caesar of a potential area over the mountains and across a desert. But before they can plan their journey, the apes' encampment is attacked in a night raid by the Army battalion Alpha-Omega and Caesar's wife and eldest son are killed.

With their location compromised, Caesar sends the apes to the new home that the scouts found, but doesn't go with them. Wanting revenge for the deaths of his family, Caesar decides to go after the Alpha-Omega colonel who led the attack. However, Maurice and Rocket refuse to let him go off on his own and join him. Before long they come upon a human child hiding in a cabin; and with no one around to care for her, Maurice takes her with them. They also encounter a gorilla named Winter who has joined the Alpha-Omegas. When questioned, he reveals that the Alpha-Omegas have relocated to a new base.

After a long trek, Caesar and his group find the new Alpha-Omega base and discover that they have captured the apes that Caesar left behind and are using them as slave labor. While scouting the base, Caesar is captured and taken to the Colonel; who tells Caesar that the Simian Flu has mutated and is now causing humans to lose the ability to speak and diminishes their mental acuity. Furthermore, the Colonel claims to be on a holy war to save humanity by eliminating the virus and all who carry it, and that it is not the apes that he's at war with, but the U.S. Army—which sees him and his battalion as war criminals committing genocide.

Caesar is then put to work with the rest of the apes, and when he tries to organize a resistance he is brutally beaten. Rocket, Maurice, and a rogue chimpanzee that has joined them named Bad Ape continue to scout the base from the outside, and eventually discover an underground tunnel. Together with Caesar they formulate a plan to free the imprisoned apes.

When the U.S. Army arrives and launches their attack on the Alpha-Omega base, the apes use the diversion as cover to assist in their escape. During the battle, the Colonel is stricken by the mutated Simian Flu and an avalanche wipes out both the U.S. Army and Alpha-Omega forces; allowing the apes to escape to the forest without being followed. However, Caesar is mortally wounded during the escape. After a long journey the apes arrive at a lake surrounded by trees beneath a mountain range. When Caesar sits down to rest, Maurice notices that his wounds have opened up and that he's been bleeding, and while they watch the apes settle into their new home Caesar quietly passes away.

REVIEW

Unfortunately *War for the Planet of the Apes*, while a good film, isn't able to match the thrills and complex storytelling of the previous two entries in the series. The name itself sets audiences up for disappointment—as the film doesn't deliver a war for planetary domination. With the last film ending on an impending all-out fight between the apes and the military, settling back into a travel film with Caesar going from place to place looking for the man who killed his family is a letdown.

The plot may be a little lackluster, but the cast isn't. Woody Harrelson delivers a memorable performance as the Colonel and Steve Zahn brings a nice bit of light humor as Bad Ape. However, it's newcomer Amiah Miller as Nova who stands out most. Child actors are notoriously problematic, and re-envisioning the Nova character as a mute child on the side of the apes had the potential to upset fans of the original film. Yet either through skilled directing or her own talent, Miller is able to engender the compassion and sympathy of the audience while still being a strong character.

And although the film doesn't deliver as much action as one would want, when the fight sequences come they are exciting and dynamic. Whether it's a group of soldiers hunting the apes through the forests, or a full on military assault with tanks and gun turrets, the action is intense and full of thrills. The final battle between the U.S. Army and the Alpha-Omegas may be one of the most elaborate fight sequences of all the films, and it doesn't disappoint.

The social commentary isn't lacking either; as the film explores such issues as second class citizenship and the ethics of warfare. However, it's not as well-done or as nuanced as in the previous entries in this trilogy. Again, another disappointment. Still, the film finds fresh and interesting ways to broach these issues and doesn't just repeat what was done before.

War for the Planet of the Apes makes some daring choices and not all of them pay off. And while it may not tell the story that one would expect, it still has an interesting story to tell. Despite its flaws, it's a smart and entertaining science-fiction adventure that stays true to the spirit of the series; combining social commentary with thrilling action. Additionally, it provides a fitting conclusion to this new re-imagined trilogy that brings things full circle.

THE DIVINE SPARK

War for the Planet of the Apes finds providence at work shaping and guiding events. The apes, after wandering in the wilderness, find a safe haven—an isolated place far from humans—in which they can begin to rebuild their community. And nature, in the form of a mutated virus, appears to be clearing the way for ape dominance as the virus spreads among the human population, robbing them of the powder of speech and reducing their mental capabilities; which in-turn reduced the threat that they pose to the apes.

CHAPTER 9

Yet providence needs people who are open to divine will. Those like Caesar, who has the courage and the vision to lead the apes to a new homeland that they can call their own. And Maurice, whose compassion and caring for the orphaned Nova bridges the divide between human and ape. However, providence is but one of a myriad of issues explored in this concluding chapter of the reimagined *Apes* trilogy.

PROMISED LAND

Hunted by the human military, Caesar has led his ape community deep into the forests. But after 2 years of evading the Alpha-Omega battalion sent after them, Caesar knows that they cannot continue like this for much longer and has sent out a scouting party to look for potentially places to set up a permanent settlement. And they return with news of a place that'll be safe and secure, and allow them to build "a new home" where they "can start over." Blue Eyes tells them that "the journey is long," over mountains and a desert, "but that [that] is why the human will not find [them]."

When the apes' encampment is attacked by an Alpha-Omega strike team and Caesar's wife and eldest son are killed, Caesar decides that it's time to leave and attempt the dangerous trek to the haven his scouts discovered. The apes pack-up and begin their journey, but before they get too far they are captured by the Alpha-Omega battalion and are taken to a work camp. And Caesar, who had left to go on his own mission, is also captured when he tracks the Alpha-Omegas to their base and comes upon the imprisoned apes. But Caesar secretly communicates with several apes on the outside who evaded capture, and they begin to work on an escape plan.

Scripture tell us that God raised up leaders to deliver His people to a choice land, an inheritance that He intended for them and blessed. It took time and faith, but God fulfilled His promise.

- Genesis 12:1-2 – *The Lord had said to Abram, "Go from your country, your people and your father's household to the land I will show you. I will make you into a great nation, and I will bless you; I will make your name great, and you will be a blessing."*

- Genesis 28:13 – *There above it stood the Lord, and he said: "I am the Lord, the God of your father Abraham and the God of Isaac. I will give you and your descendants the land on which you are lying."*

- Leviticus 20:24 – *I said to you, "You will possess their land; I will give it to you as an inheritance, a land flowing with milk and honey." I am the Lord your God, who has set you apart from the nations.*

- Judges 2:1 – *The angel of the Lord went up from Gilgal to Bokim and said, "I brought you up out of Egypt and led you into the land I swore to give to your ancestors. I said, 'I will never break my covenant with you,'"*

Using an underground tunnel, the apes escape from the base. And when the Alpha-Omegas come under attack from the U.S. Army, they use the opportunity to

CHAPTER 9

make their way to a nearby mountain side while the soldiers are distracted. From there, Caesar leads his people across barren and hostile terrain and finally arrives at a lake surrounded by a forest at the base of a mountain—a safe place far from any human settlements.

CARING FOR ORPHANS

After leaving the apes to seek his revenge on the Alpha-Omegas, Caesar is joined by a handful of his closest friends, including Maurice and Rocket. Along their journey they come across a human soldier and are forced to kill him when he pulls a gun on them. They then secure the area and discover a small child who is unable to speak. With no other humans around to care for the child, Maurice takes it upon himself to look after her; telling Caesar that, "She'll die out here alone" and that he "cannot leave her."

As they travel, Maurice teaches the young girl sign language and the two start to bond. By the time they get to the Alpha-Omega base, the apes have come to see the child as one of their own and decide to keep her with them instead of leaving her with the humans. And as they plan for the rescue of the captured apes inside the base, Maurice keeps the child by his side and sees to her safety.

We too are to care for the orphaned and abandoned. Throughout Scripture God makes it clear that mistreatment of the vulnerable is an abomination before Him, and that those who call Him Lord are to offer care and aid to those in need.

- Exodus 22:22-23 – *Do not take advantage of the widow or the fatherless. If you do and they cry out to me, I will certainly hear their cry.*

- Deuteronomy 27:19 – *Cursed is anyone who withholds justice from the foreigner, the fatherless or the widow.*

- Psalm 82:3-4 – *Defend the weak and the fatherless; uphold the cause of the poor and the oppressed. Rescue the weak and the needy; deliver them from the hand of the wicked.*

- James 1:27 – *Religion that God our Father accepts as pure and faultless is this: to look after orphans and widows in their distress and to keep oneself from being polluted by the world.*

After spending so much time with the apes, the child comes to think of herself as an ape—eventually asking Maurice if she is an ape. Knowing that she is not a normal human but not an ape either, Maurice thinks it over and tells her, "You are...Nova"—signifying her special uniqueness. And after the apes escape from the Alpha-Omega base they take her with them to their new home. Nova is welcomed into their community and is allowed to join them as they set about building a future.

EUTHANASIA

As Caesar and his friends track the Alpha-Omegas, they come across a group of dead and dying soldiers. They appear to be unable to speak and to have been shot by their own men. Later, the Colonel will tell Caesar that the Simian Flu has mutated, "[a]nd that if it spread[s]

CHAPTER 9

it [will] destroy humanity...by robbing [them] of those things that make [them] human," such as "speech [and] higher thinking." Seeing no value in living in such a state and wanting to protect humanity from becoming weak, the Colonel has ordered that anyone showing signs of the mutated Simian Flu is to be summarily killed for the good of the community.

When the Colonel's superiors learned what he had done they tried to convince him to stand down and to let the medics handle the infected. But given the failures to stop the spread of the original Simian Flu, the Colonel took drastic action—killing his superiors—and refused to give up his command or his mission to save humanity. He tells Caesar that sparing the infected from living as primitives is "mercy." However, the U.S. Army sees it as murdering innocents and mounts a force to stop the genocidal killing of the infected that the Colonel and his Alpha-Omega battalion are engaging in.

Scripture teaches us that our lives and our deaths are in God's hands. He is our Creator, and He has the right to determine when our time here on earth has come to its end. And to attempt to assume that control goes against His will.

- Deuteronomy 32:39 – *See now that I myself am he! There is no god besides me. I put to death and I bring to life, I have wounded and I will heal, and no one can deliver out of my hand.*

- Job 12:10 – *In his hand is the life of every creature and the breath of all mankind.*

- Job 14:5 – *A person's days are determined; you have decreed the number of his months and have set limits he cannot exceed.*

- 1 Corinthians 6:19-20 – *Do you not know that your bodies are temples of the Holy Spirit, who is in you, whom you have received from God? You are not your own; you were bought at a price. Therefore honor God with your bodies.*

After finding Nova's ragdoll in Caesar cage, the Colonel contracts the mutated virus—turning him into the very thing that he has sought to destroy. When Caesar goes to the Colonel's quarters to kill him during the battle with the Army, he finds the Colonel lying in bed unable to speak. Looking at Caesar, the Colonel places Caesar's gun to his forehead; asking for a mercy killing. But in that moment Caesar overcomes his anger and vengeance. Instead, he looks at the Colonel with compassion and lowers his gun, not wanting any more needless killing, and keeps to his moral code that mercy is sparing life, not taking it.

ALPHA AND OMEGA

It's often hard for us to see God's guiding hand leading us on in life's journey. The hard times especially can cause us to doubt His divine plan or question if there even is one. Yet in hind-sight, when the time of tribulation has passed, it becomes easier to see how we were being prepared for things to come, saved from a wrong path, or needed to wait for certain events to unfold. Life moves at an ever increasing pace, but God will not be rushed. As American evangelist Charles Swindall once said, "God's timing is always on time."

We are not when and where we are by accident. Like the Israelites of old, God is still leading His people to promised lands. They may not be physical lands, but God is still guiding us to the places we need to be in order to prosper and carry out His will. We will not always know why He guides us to the places He does, especially when we encounter hardship, but God has plans for each and every one of us. And His plans, while not always clear, are for our good and will help us to become the people He promised we could be in communion and service to Him.

All life is precious to God, for "[t]hrough him all things were made" (John 1:3). And we have been called to protect and care for that life. In Christ's ministry He spoke extensively about caring for the weak and vulnerable; particularly the infirmed and the orphan—those who society is most readily willing to undervalue and dismiss. Therefore it's our duty to look past the worth society puts on a life and see all life as inherently valuable and a reflection of the Creator.

God's plans are always active in our lives, even when we can't see them, for He is always with us. Yet we are not hapless bystanders resigned to a fate that we have no control over. We have a role to play and responsibilities to fulfil in the plans that God has. And if we follow His word and serve Him to the best of our ability, then He is sure to bless us and see us through to the place He has prepared for us among the saints and the heavenly hosts.

Jeremiah 29:11 – *"For I know the plans I have for you," declares the* L<small>ORD</small>, *"plans to prosper you and not to harm you, plans to give you hope and a future."*

"[I]n the fullness of time, evil men betrayed God's trust, and in disobedience to His holy word waged bloody wars..."

CONCLUSION

Is it any wonder that the Planet of the Apes franchise became a cultural phenomenon? From when the first film was released in 1968 to the present, they have spoken to the issues of their day. And not just the larger cultural and political issues, but the things that people dealt with in their everyday lives. While the "Planet" title may allude to a far-off space adventure in the stars, the audience comes to discover the same thing that Col. Taylor does in the first film's climax, "I'm home. All the time..."—the stories have been about us.

Of course, it's common for science-fiction to use aliens and other worlds as a guise to make social commentary. *Planet of the Apes* is only one such example. What would be provocative and inflammatory as a modern day drama becomes acceptable in a science-fiction and fantasy veneer. And *Apes* does this masterfully. Whether it's race relations or genetic engineering, *Apes* has always found a way to defuse social and political issues of their more confrontational elements and to use allegories that can be seen by those looking for it, or overlooked by those who just focus on the adventure story (though to be fair, not every *Apes* film succeeds at this).

But do the messages within these films stop there? To think so would be rather naïve, would it not? As discussed previously, the *Apes* films are the product of many talented individuals and artisans; from the producers to the writers to the actors to the set designers and effects crews—each contributing to the vision that became the Planet of the Apes saga.

What a character's makeup and costume conveys about them can go beyond what is in the script. And how an actor interprets and embodies a character can entirely change how they are viewed. And a film's musical score can often do more to set a mood than the lighting or camera angels. Now this is not to say that these different elements are presenting different visions of the material. In fact, they usually work in concert to enhance and support the themes and tones of the film. Yet when looked at in isolation, they can be doing and saying more than what was intended.

Additionally, in retrospect a film says much about the time and culture in which it was made. While not intended, a film is full of messages about the cultural norms and social mores of its time: the roles men and women play, the types of behavior that people engage in, the way societal institutions are portrayed. And its juxtaposition against where we are now says something as well; about what we have lost and what we have gained, how we have advanced or regressed, how society has shifted. Of particular interest in the genre of dystopian science-fiction (like the *Apes* series) is how it reveals our fears—nuclear war in the 20th century and viral outbreaks in the 21st.

Given all of this, it is safe to say that there is more to the *Apes* films than a surface reading would suggest. But are there moral messages and are they in keeping with the teachings of the bible? I would say "Yes" on both counts.

CONCLUSION

As strange as it may sound, the *Apes* films are morality tales. While their endings are usually dower, it's often a comeuppance for the perpetrating of evil; whether it's Taylor discovering that mankind destroyed itself or Governor Breck witnessing the enslaved apes overthrow their oppressors. There's a strong sense of morality in the world of Planet of the Apes—at least when it comes to punishing those who do evil.

But more than that, the continuing themes throughout the films about the evils of violence and the injustice of prejudice are tenets of the Christian faith. Christ taught that those who live by the sword will die by the sword (Matthew 26:52), and this is dramatized repeatedly in the films—and quite effectively (hence the resonance of the image of the destroyed Statue of Liberty). And Christ and His disciples fought against the ethnic prejudices of their day; offering salvation to Jew and Gentile, and teaching that all are brothers in Christ (Galatians 3:28). Similarly, the hero characters of the *Apes* films, Zira, Armando, Caesar, are the ones who treat apes and humans as equals and fight for equality.

Additionally, the Apes' most sacred rule is "Ape shall never kill ape"—a clear allusion to the biblical commandment that "Thou shall not kill" (Exodus 20:13, King James Version). Caesar leads his people out of slavery—a direct allegory to Moses. And Dr. Hasslein attempts to hunt down and kill Caesar in his infancy—a Christ allegory. The biblical influences in the Planet of the Apes films are numerous and unmistakable.

Of course there are messages within the films that are not biblical and are even contrary to Scripture. The films, after all, are science-fiction adventures about giant intelligent apes in a distant future or alternate reality. To expect them to adhere solely to Judeo-Christian theology would be foolish. Even Christian authors make certain allowances in their science-fiction and fantasy works. But I believe on the whole it can be said that the *Apes* films depict Judeo-Christian morality.

Some will disagree with this assessment (and they are free to do so), but I believe that looking at the *Apes* films from a Judeo-Christian morality perspective makes for an interesting viewing experience. When watched in this way, one will begin to see the characters and stories in a new light. Perhaps even gain a new appreciation of the series and what it has to say about life, morality, and the human condition. One may even begin to view issues of faith differently after seeing them presented in the context of these films.

As a Christian I find the Planet of the Apes series affirming, as it reflects my Christian beliefs on numerous issues; from forgiveness to prayer to fellowship to sacrifice. It also has many cautionary lessons about the abuse of religion, false prophets, and blind faith. The *Apes* criticisms of religion are as valid and instructional as its extollings of its virtues. The films have never been shy about exploring the dark and ugly side of society and humanity, and Christians need to be ever vigilant that we are not corrupted by the world or turn a blind eye to its transgressions against the will of God.

Some will watch the Planet of the Apes films for entertainment and leave it at that. But I contend that they have more to say, and, that for Christians in particular, they can be used to explore and discuss issues of faith. Scripture tells us that "God chose the foolish things of the world to shame the wise" (1 Corinthians 1:27), and

CONCLUSION

what could be more foolish than a monkey movie? A monkey movie would be just the sort of thing God would use to entertain, challenge, and enlighten the faithful. Science-fiction/fantasy parables for a new age. As Dr. Zaius would say, "Keep digging…You'll find the master of this house"—God…on the Planet of the Apes.

BIBLIOGRAPHY

Crossway Bibles, "Topical Bible". 2001. OpenBible.info.

Burton, Tim, dir. *Planet of the Apes*; 2001; Beverly Hills, CA: Twentieth Century Fox Home Entertainment, 2001. DVD

Post, Ted, dir. *Beneath the Planet of the Apes*; 1970; Beverly Hills, CA: Twentieth Century Fox Home Entertainment, 2008. Blu-ray

Reeves, Matt, dir. *Dawn of the Planet of the Apes*; 2014; Beverly Hills, CA: Twentieth Century Fox Home Entertainment, 2014. Blu-ray

Reeves, Matt, dir. *War for the Planet of the Apes*; 2017; Beverly Hills, CA: Twentieth Century Fox Home Entertainment, 2017. Blu-ray

Schaffner, Franklin J., dir. *Planet of the Apes*; 1968; Beverly Hills, CA: Twentieth Century Fox Home Entertainment, 2008. Blu-ray

Taylor, Don, dir. *Escape from the Planet of the Apes*; 1971; Beverly Hills, CA: Twentieth Century Fox Home Entertainment, 2008. Blu-ray

Thompson, J. Lee, dir. *Battle for the Planet of the Apes*; 1973; Beverly Hills, CA: Twentieth Century Fox Home Entertainment, 2008. Blu-ray

Thompson, J. Lee, dir. *Conquest of the Planet of the Apes*; 1972; Beverly Hills, CA: Twentieth Century Fox Home Entertainment, 2008. Blu-ray

Wyatt, Rupert, dir. *Rise of the Planet of the Apes*; 2011; Beverly Hills, CA: Twentieth Century Fox Home Entertainment, 2011. Blu-ray

Zondervan Corporation. BibleGateway.com. 1995-2023.

www.ingramcontent.com/pod-product-compliance
Lightning Source LLC
LaVergne TN
LVHW061038070526
838201LV00073B/5090